# The
# EVERYTHING.
## Screenwriting Book

Dear Reader:

The first published piece I was paid for on my way to becoming a professional writer was an article for an English movie magazine called *Picturegoer*. That was many, many years ago. If you think I like movies and how they are made, you're right. I even wrote the first-draft screenplay based on my own novel *Loophole or How to Rob a Bank* that starred Albert Finney and Martin Sheen. (You'll find out in this book what they mean in the industry by "first draft.")

Writing this book took me back to studios in Hollywood and London, England, and to the people I used to know there. It also took me to the University of California at Berkeley, where I was writing and directing films as the director of multimedia.

We all have our favorite memories about movies that for one reason or another mean something special to us. So, for me to write a book about how they are written was a treat. I hope you like it as much as I enjoyed writing it.

Most sincerely,

# The EVERYTHING® Series

## Editorial

| | |
|---|---|
| Publishing Director | Gary M. Krebs |
| Managing Editor | Kate McBride |
| Copy Chief | Laura MacLaughlin |
| Acquisitions Editor | Bethany Brown |
| Development Editor | Julie Gutin |
| Production Editor | Khrysti Nazzaro |

## Production

| | |
|---|---|
| Production Director | Susan Beale |
| Production Manager | Michelle Roy Kelly |
| Series Designers | Daria Perreault |
| | Colleen Cunningham |
| Cover Design | Paul Beatrice |
| | Frank Rivera |
| Layout and Graphics | Colleen Cunningham |
| | Rachael Eiben |
| | Michelle Roy Kelly |
| | Daria Perreault |
| | Erin Ring |
| Series Cover Artist | Barry Littmann |

**Visit the entire Everything® Series at everything.com**

# THE
# EVERYTHING®
# SCREENWRITING
# BOOK

From developing a treatment to
writing and selling your script—
all you need to perfect your craft

Robert Pollock

Adams Media Corporation
Avon, Massachusetts

An Everything® Series Book.
Everything® and everything.com® are registered trademarks of F+W Publications, Inc.

Published by Adams Media, an F+W Publications Company
57 Littlefield Street, Avon, MA 02322 U.S.A.
*www.adamsmedia.com*

ISBN: 1-58062-955-5
Printed in the United States of America.

J I H G F E D C

**Library of Congress Cataloging-in-Publication Data**
Pollock, Robert.
The everything screenwriting book / Robert Pollock.
p.    cm.
(An everything series)
ISBN 1-58062-955-5
1. Motion picture authorship. I. Title. II. Series.
PN1996.P64 2003
808.2'3—dc21
2003008262

This publication is designed to provide accurate and authoritative information with regard to the subject matter covered. It is sold with the understanding that the publisher is not engaged in rendering legal, accounting, or other professional advice. If legal advice or other expert assistance is required, the services of a competent professional person should be sought.
—From a *Declaration of Principles* jointly adopted by a Committee of the American Bar Association and a Committee of Publishers and Associations

Many of the designations used by manufacturers and sellers to distinguish their products are claimed as trademarks. Where those designations appear in this book and Adams Media was aware of a trademark claim, the designations have been printed with initial capital letters.

*This book is available at quantity discounts for bulk purchases.*
*For information, call 1-800-872-5627.*

# Contents

# Dedication

This book is dedicated to Susan E. Craig, M.D.,
for all her wonderful help and encouragement.

# Top Ten Points
## To Writing the Perfect Screenplay

1. Try to come up with a unique story idea—Hollywood is always looking for the next original hit.

2. Pay attention to organization; your script should be divided into three acts, with an introduction, plot points, climax, and resolution.

3. Avoid stereotypical characters; the characters you create should undergo character development as the action progresses.

4. Once you know what kind of movie you'd like to write, get inspiration from similar movies.

5. Keep your audience in mind; film audiences today have certain expectations. For instance, a romantic comedy always has a happy ending.

6. Write about what you know—and if you don't, make sure you do some research.

7. Keep in mind that writing a screenplay is all about combining what you see and what you hear, and putting it down on paper.

8. Find an attentive friend to give you critical feedback as a potential viewer, or, better yet, form a screenwriting group.

9. Remember that writing is about rewriting—don't be afraid to cut and start from scratch.

10. Once you've finished your screenplay, your work is only half done. Now it's time to find an agent and try to get a film contract to transform a script into a movie.

# *Introduction*

▶ UNLIKE ALMOST ALL OTHER FORMS OF WRITING, you don't need any literary talent to write for the movies or television. What you do need is a well-developed visual imagination and a good working knowledge of how the movie business works. As John Seabrook reported in the *New Yorker*, George Lucas took about two years to write the first draft of his screenplay. He used regular No. 2 pencils and wrote in tiny, compulsively neat-looking script on green-and-blue-lined paper. His spelling was apparently atrocious and his grammar a joke. Well, we all know what that lousy spelling and grammar led to—*Star Wars*.

As Ernest Hemingway is reputed to have said, you can always pay someone to fix the spelling and put the commas in the right places. But on the other hand, it's not a bad idea to remember that it's a good worker who knows his tools. A good carpenter knows which chisel to take up and a good artist knows how to mix his or her oils and so on. It's the same with writing—if you get to know the rules, you will know how to break them and often that's where the originality springs from, although as far as today's movies and television are concerned, perhaps it wouldn't hurt to go easy on the originality.

While taking classes in film production and screenwriting certainly shouldn't do any harm, keep in mind that, according to biographer Marion Meade, Woody Allen barely passed the motion-picture production course he took at New York University and was subsequently kicked out.

Films and television are so much a part of all our lives and the society in which we live that to have the ambition to be a part of them by making the words you write contribute to their production is a wonderful aim. To sit in a movie theater and look up at the screen as the credits roll by and see your name up there as the writer is a thrill that truly makes all the hard work and the risk of rejection worthwhile. That's what this book is about—the fun and wonder of writing successfully for the movies or television.

Relatively speaking, the history of the movies is a short one. Less than a hundred years ago, in 1927, the silent era ended and sound was born when Al Jolson spoke the words, "You ain't heard nothing yet" in the Warner Bros. picture *The Jazz Singer*. From that moment on, someone would have to write the words for actors to say. The modern screenplay came into being.

Movies have been influencing people ever since the first fluttering black-and-white images appeared on a white screen. They have a bearing on how people think, dress, act, and speak. Film production has provided employment to millions worldwide, to say nothing of the millions earned at the box office.

This book will take you into the world of the movies—the world of creativity and drama—and teach you how to get inside that world if you work hard and persevere. It should never be forgotten that without the screenwriter there would be nothing up there on the screen.

## Chapter 1

# Historical Outline of the Movies

To get a handle on what's happening in the movies today and how you can become a part of the moviemaking process, it's necessary to have a working knowledge of how the film industry came about and developed. The aspiring screenwriter needs to know what contributed over the years to the technically sophisticated productions showing down the street at the local multiplex. It's an exciting story.

# Invention of the Motion-Picture Camera

Although there's a commonly held belief that Thomas Edison invented the motion-picture camera, in fact the U.S. Supreme Court concluded in 1902 that a number of individuals throughout the world were involved in its invention and development. One of these contributors was Edison's own assistant, W.K.L. Dickson. Together, Edison and his staff developed a motion-picture camera that they called the Kinetograph.

**FACT**

The Kinetoscope was commercially marketed and installed in amusement parks, penny arcades, and other places of public recreation. The first Kinetoscope parlor opened in 1894 in New York City and patrons were charged twenty-five cents for admission. It wasn't long until these parlors were dubbed peepshows.

The motion-picture camera was only the first step in the process because it operated without a projector; to view the moving pictures, you had to peek into a black box where a loop of film ran on a spool between an incandescent lamp and a shutter. Edison named this early contraption the Kinetoscope.

## How It Works

Films are made of still pictures called *frames* that flicker onto the screen at a speed of twenty-four frames a second. Because the changes happen too fast for the human eye to notice, what we see is an illusion of the moving image. The film in a movie camera is exposed behind a lens. A shutter stops the light from reaching the film as it unrolls from a supply reel on its way to move intermittently through a gate in the camera, which is where the exposure takes place. Then, it travels on to the take-up reel.

The one component of the movie camera (as well as the still camera) that has undergone continuous evolvement is the lens. Today, camera lenses are much better at attaining sharp focus in a wide variety of focal lengths aimed to get the best results, all the way from ultrawide angle to telephoto.

It was only seventy-five years ago that a movie cameraman had to wrap his camera in a blanket to mute the sound it made so that the microphone wouldn't pick it up. Microphones were often hidden close to the actors but, of course, out of sight of the camera.

# Growth of the Film-Production Industry

The peepshows were making money, but they needed a never-ending supply of new pictures (product) for the customers to view. It was a logical move, therefore, for Edison to get into the production business. In 1901, Edison opened a small studio in New York, where live vaudeville or circus acts were brought in and recorded.

Because Edison didn't file any international patents, anyone could copy and make motion-picture equipment. This led to immediate improvements. At a Kinetoscope exhibition in Paris, Auguste and Louis Lumière got the idea to invent a film projector, which they called a Cinématographe. The original battery-driven Kinetoscope weighed a hefty 1,000 pounds; the hand-cranked Cinématographe a mere twenty pounds, providing portability.

The movie industry moved ahead with some speed as entrepreneurs came to see the possibilities of producing motion pictures and earning income from their distribution. Europe took a lead in production and exhibition. Beginning in 1905, one production company set up in the small middle-class seaside town of Brighton, England, was turning out up to fifty films a year. Producers were at work experimenting with a rudimentary form of editing and even primitive special effects—superimpositions and close-ups.

## A Dose of Healthy Competition

Edison faced competition at home as well. The most successful rival was D. W. Griffith and his company, Biograph. Around this time, the system of distribution had gained in sophistication; instead of selling films for exhibition, the production company would create a leasing arrangement and set up rental fees based on production costs and box-office receipts.

In the early film industry, the most important and powerful source of light was the sun. Studios were designed to revolve so they could follow it. The lack of a reliable sun was the main reason for the relocation of New York studios to sunny Southern California.

## Production Values

As money poured into the business, the producers saw the need for improved production values. At that time, scripts were generally in the hands of the directors, who basically broke down whatever story they had into a series of shots. (Little attention was paid to character development and motivation.)

The breakdown of shots was primitive and impulsive; words such as *cut, dissolve, close-up,* and so on had not yet entered the production lexicon. Griffith apparently worked by instinct, which often meant shooting what today would be considered stagelike tableaus, rather like sticking the actors up against a static background and shooting away without any thought beyond simple composition.

## Turning Up the Sound

Early sounds in the cinema were very simple. They consisted of a record player that would play a record, a system called sound-on-disk. It was that system that was used in the first commercial film with sound—the 1927 film *The Jazz Singer* from Warner Bros. The sound was recorded after the film was shot and the record was then played on a turntable that synchronized the sound with the film by controlling the speed of the projector.

The next step forward was sound-on-film, which came in the early 1930s. The technique was to have the soundtrack running along one side of the 35mm film stock. You could pick up a length of 35mm film, hold it up to the light, and see the soundtrack. Very simply put, the film projector had an optical pickup head that read the track and sent the sound to speakers located behind the screen. Because the sound had to travel from the projector to the speakers, the soundtracks on the film were printed several frames away from their related images to accommodate the delay.

If the film broke and had to be spliced back together with a couple of frames missing, and if the projectionist doing the repair did not work to the calibration markings on the film, then it might very well be out of sync; the sound and the lip movements wouldn't match.

Once the captions of the silent films gave way to sound, filmmakers realized it could be used to create suspense. Show the audience a villain walking a dark, wet street and let them hear his footsteps. Then cut to an empty street around the corner. There's nothing to see, but you can hear the footsteps coming closer. And you know something is about to happen.

Sound brought the potential for tremendous added drama to motion pictures—the ticking of a time bomb, the whisper of a lover's words, the squeaking of a door, the sound of falling rain, a scream. Every sound that's ever been made can be written into a screenplay to be captured on film.

## Sound Development

The next step in technical sound advancement was the development of multichannel soundtracks. In 1940, at the premiere of Walt Disney's *Fantasia,* special sound equipment was installed at the screening site— New York's Broadway Theater. The contraption was called Fantasound and consisted of multidirectional speakers that had been distributed throughout the theater. Leopold Stokowski, the creator of the movie's soundtrack, recorded an optical track for each section of the orchestra. There were nine separate soundtracks mixed into four master optical tracks. The system was not only elaborate, it was very costly, and it stagnated until 1990, when it was remastered in Dolby 70mm magnetic 4 track matrix stereo sound.

The most famous sound studio in the business is George Lucas's Skywalker Sound in Marin County, California, which is part of Industrial Light and Magic. It was started back in the early 1980s and was responsible for creating the sound effects for the *Star Wars* movies, among many others.

Further advancement of sound systems in movies was not hampered by technical inability so much as economics. In most cases, the costs of re-equipping existing exhibition theaters with new sound systems were prohibitive.

# The Evolution of Sound Effects

If the sound effects of a modern blockbuster film like *Men in Black* were somehow obliterated from the film, it's doubtful whether the movie would get an exhibition date, let alone a sizable audience. Sound effects, just like special visual effects, have become an accepted essential in today's made-for-mass-distribution movies.

In spite of the many systems of sending sound from a film into the viewing theater, and with all their esoteric names and descriptions, it is not just the quality of the sound that is being distributed but its content that is of importance to the film and its reception by the audience. The old computer saying "garbage in, garbage out" could well be used in reference to movie sounds.

## Recording Sounds

Having sound in a movie is not just a case of sticking some microphones around the studio or a location. A sound mixer (recordist) has to differentiate the recorded sounds. If you put a tape recorder outside your back door and hit the record button, the recorder will record all the sounds it detects—a lot more than your ears, because we all filter out as much of the unnecessary sounds as we can.

Sound in a movie is recorded both as the movie is being shot and later in a sound studio. Sounds are added; sounds are deleted. Sometimes sounds or dialogue are replaced because of some distortion on the original take. Doing this used to be called *looping.* On location, where sound cannot be controlled, a sound technician would record "wild" sound, also called *ambient sound,* which would be added to the track later in the postproduction phase.

**What does "looping" mean and do?**
Looping involves rerecording the actors' dialogue in a studio so as to replace some distortion in the original take. Today looping has been replaced by ADR (Automatic Dialogue Replacement).

**QUESTION?**

## Sound Engineering

Very broadly speaking, it could be said that there are two kinds of movie sounds: "real" sounds and "created/invented." Real sounds are, obviously, things like the dialogue actors utter, the sounds of real life, and so on. Created, or invented, sounds would be the sound of a supersonic laser gun being fired in a sci-fi movie, or the sound of a created animal as it's about to eat the heroine.

The job of sound engineers, who work in a highly trained team, is to select and modify sounds that match what is being seen on the screen as well as the background music. Sound engineering is a hi-tech job, and there's an Oscar presented each year for Best Sound. Hi-tech blockbusters couldn't do without it.

## Fixing Sounds

For example, let's say the script calls for a cocktail party where one of the characters drops a wineglass, which smashes on a stone floor. The sound is recorded live as the scene is shot; in postproduction, that sound together with thousands of others has to be correctly and dramatically balanced.

If the live sound has some kind of defect, the sound department has to come up with the perfect sound from the sound library. In the unlikely event that the sound of a breaking wineglass isn't available, the sound department has to create/invent it in the studio. Think of the old trick of coconut shell halves being banged together to make for a horse galloping; the principle is the same.

**FACT**

Most major studios have exhaustive sound libraries, and there are a number of independent sound libraries as well. There is a kind of magic to manipulating sound in movies.

## The Arrival of Color

Today, we take color films for granted; only a few art films are still shot in black and white. But color filmmaking didn't just happen. Like all technical innovations in motion pictures, it was a gradual process of development.

As far back as 1855, people have been conducting experiments to produce color films by filming three separate black-and-white negatives through red, green, and blue filters (these three colors are known as the primary colors). In the mid-1900s, some began to use stencils. Later still, stencils were replaced by mechanized tinting and toning.

It wasn't until the 1930s that Technicolor, which had a virtual monopoly with its system, reached the stage where color films made the jump into major production. Some of the most famous Technicolor productions are *Snow White and the Seven Dwarfs* (1936), *The Adventures of Robin Hood* (1938), *The Wizard of Oz* (1939), and *Gone with the Wind* (1939).

**ESSENTIAL**

Of the various competing systems for color, only Technicolor film permanently retains its original colors. Other color prints fade to magenta within seven years, which has proved to be a problem for film preservationists. The Technicolor hard gelatin dyes remain undimmed.

# Expansion of Format

In the 1950s, television exploded into color and even came with remote controls. The film industry was sent into a spin and, as a reaction to the sit-at-home competition, came up with new techniques for both making and showing movies. The theory was to provide scope and public entertainment, which would pry people off their sofas and out into the cinemas.

As often happens when people rush to change, the results weren't as successful as originally envisaged. This was the case when a selection of movie formats came about. It was a prime example of how attention to form can replace the importance of content.

# CinemaScope

The size and shape of most movie screens in the 1950s was roughly 4 to 3 or 1.33 to 1 (this is known as the *aspect ratio,* or the ratio of frame width to frame height). But in the 1920s, a French physicist named Henri Chrétien invented a process that relied on a special lens (called an *anamorphic lens*) to squeeze a wide picture onto a standard 35mm film, making the figures appear tall and thin. A lens on the projector reversed the effect, so that the images on the screen took on their normal proportions. But the system produced a different ratio: an image with a width 2½ times its height. The system was called CinemaScope.

**ALERT!**

When older films shot in CinemaScope are shown on television today, they are cropped to accommodate the images on the TV screen. Sometimes, right at the end of the film when the credits come up, you can see the elongated figures, because that section of the film had not been adjusted.

The Twentieth Century Fox Film corporation acquired the rights to CinemaScope and the first CinemaScope picture from Fox went into production and premiered in 1953. *The Robe,* starring Richard Burton, Jean Simmons, and Victor Mature, was based on the religious book of the same name by Lloyd C. Douglas. The screenplay was written by Philip Dunne and directed by Henry Koster.

## Other Production Formats

CinemaScope wasn't the only big-screen format that the studios used in their efforts to attract audiences into the cinemas. A three-projector system called Cinerama used a wide curved screen and a separate seven-track magnetic soundtrack. Only specially equipped Cinerama theaters could exhibit films made for this system.

Because the equipment for making Cinerama films was expensive, only a few films appeared in this format. *This Is Cinerama* (1952) was the first release; *Seven Wonders of the World* (1956) and *How the West Was Won* (1962) are two other examples.

*Oklahoma!* was shot two ways: in Todd AO and in CinemaScope. Some of the scenes were actually filmed differently. In other cases, where it was practical, two cameras were set up next to each other and joint filming was done at the same time. All three original Todd AO productions were screened and are available in other formats like CinemaScope.

In 1955, Michael Todd (then husband of Elizabeth Taylor) introduced yet another format, called Todd AO. This time, the screen image was on a curved screen that was 13 feet deep in the center and 50 feet wide by 25 feet high. The first production was *Oklahoma!,* with Gordon MacRae, Shirley Jones, and Rod Steiger. Two other Todd AO films were made: *Around the World in 80 Days* (1955) and *South Pacific* (1958).

## The Ultimate Screening Experience

Three-dimensional (3-D) formats aren't exactly new; stereoscope viewing was in vogue way back in the mid-1800s. The first motion pictures in 3-D were created by Englishman William Friese-Greene around 1889. After that time, the interest in 3-D formats grew and waned.

In the 1950s, when the industry was looking for fresh production techniques that would prompt patrons to head for the cinema, Warner Bros. released what has become a cult film of the 3-D genre: *House of Wax*. The film starred the actor who became the master of horror films, Vincent Price. It also featured Phyllis Kirk and Charles Bronson.

Edwin H. Land of Polaroid fame had a hand in the production and viewing system—his light-polarizing material was involved in the recording and projection of two films with lens that polarized light at different angles. Polarized spectacles were given to spectators to wear while viewing the film, which created the appearance of three-dimensional depth.

# The New World of Special Effects

The basic principle of special effects is how to show an image or scene that didn't actually take place in real life, even though it may look absolutely real onscreen. For instance, how did they make the DeLorean car in *Back to the Future* fly down Main Street?

There are several processes used to achieve these effects, and all are in wide use in the motion picture/television industry. They are a *double-exposure matte, traveling matte* (or *blue-screen technique*), and *morphing*. These techniques allow actors, television newscasters, and scale models to stay in the studio while appearing to be dangling from a skyscraper, zooming through the air like Spiderman, or standing thousands of miles away in the middle of the Australian outback.

## Double-Exposure Matte

Here's how this relatively simple process works. First, the actors are shot while performing—for instance, crawling over a plain in the desert—while a sheet of black paper or black tape is placed over the top horizontal half of the camera lens. After the shot is made, the camera is rewound. The cameraman moves the black tape to cover the bottom half of the lens and shoots a stormy, lightning-filled sky at slow film speed.

Because the sky section was filmed at slow speed, the result will be a very fast moving lightning storm passing over two men in a desert. The shot of the sky does not have to be of a real one; today it can be computer generated.

## Traveling Mattes

Traveling mattes allow the director to film dangerous shots without putting the stars in any danger or relying on stunt doubles. Instead, the director may use the blue-screen technique.

The action is performed in front of a background screen, which is colored a bright blue. The actual scene is shot separately. Then, technicians take over and marry the two shots. So, for instance, you can film your star actress walking against the blue screen, then film a shot of a shaky bridge above a raging river; by combining the two shots, you'll see the star traversing that bridge. Today, the process of making the shots is considerably easier and quicker because of the help filmmakers get from computer technologies.

**ALERT!**

It is vital that the actor in a blue-screen shot doesn't wear anything that is colored blue. If she or he does, the part covered by the blue clothing will show up as a hole in the actor's body.

The blue-screen technique has been and is still used extensively in all science fiction films. The entire process has become very sophisticated. The point of it all is to convince the viewer that what he or she sees up on the screen is really happening.

## Morphing

Morphing is a technique for transferring one image into another. Early films that used morphing to great effect were *The Mask* and *Terminator 2: Judgment Day*. In the music video industry, Michael Jackson's *Black and White* relied on pioneering use of morphing.

Unlike other forms of special visual effects, morphing has a limited application, mainly because the audience can see the change from "real" to "special effect." In fact, its whole attraction is drawing attention to itself as if to say, look at what I can do. If a film overuses this technique, it risks boring its audience.

## Why Do People Go to the Cinema?

There are countless books and articles that attempt to analyze the reasons why we all go to the cinema. Some people are attracted—and sometimes even obsessed by—the leading actor or actress. Some use movies to escape the harsh realities of life. Others have more mundane reasons, like a way to socialize with friends or even finding an air-conditioned place during the summer. Of course, screenwriters like to think that it's because they write such wonderful films.

While there are people who will sit and watch really terrible movies, there aren't enough of them for those movies to earn out, so movies do need to be well made. On the other hand, films that appeal to niche audiences are equally unsuccessful financial ventures—they just won't be popular enough to attract a large audience.

What kinds of movies have a large audience? One way of looking at the answer is by figuring out which movies are most frequently rented from video stores. Here is a list of ten top-selling video rentals for the year 2001 (information provided by Box Office Mojo, an online reporting service):

1. *Meet the Parents*
2. *What Women Want*
3. *Miss Congeniality*
4. *Castaway*
5. *What Lies Beneath*
6. *Me, Myself & Irene*
7. *The Family Man*
8. *Traffic*
9. *Remember the Titans*
10. *Hollow Man*

Do you see what all of these movies have in common? What conclusions can you draw about the film industry's market? Do you think your screenwriting idea will have a place among these ten?

## Chapter 2

# Introduction to Screenwriting

Writing for money is a gamble, and writing for the movie screen is an even less sure way of making a living. So why do so many people want to write screenplays? Perhaps it's because the rewards for the lucky few are substantial—money and prestige. And, of course, it's a thrill to sit back and watch a film that was born as an idea in your head and that you shaped and crafted into a screenplay.

# What Is a Screenplay?

A screenplay or film script is a blueprint from which, eventually, a motion picture will be made. This blueprint is the most important element of a film—you can't produce a film without a screenplay just as you can't construct a skyscraper without architectural blueprints.

The script includes all kinds of information, which appears both directly and indirectly. Most obviously, it contains the dialogue broken down by act, scene, and shot. However, to arrive at the screenplay, the screenwriter will already have decided how long the film will be, where it will be shot, how many actors will be needed, and so on. This type of indirect information is equally important.

A screenplay is never a work of literature, something one person writes and another reads. It is a blueprint for something that is heard, seen, and interpreted by a viewer.

## From Script to Successful Motion Picture

Although most scripts are written by only one person, it requires hundreds of professionals to make a script into a film. To organize the venture, the project must have a leader. In the movies, this is the role of the director.

ESSENTIAL

The cinematographer, sound designer and engineers, set and costume designers, editors, composers and musicians, and others working on film production generally receive a copy of the script of the movie they are working on.

## The Screenwriter Plays God

Which of the platoon's heroes will die? The comic who is always cracking jokes, the serious lieutenant who always worries about his family back home, the unrelenting sadistic sergeant who is ready to lead his men into battle? It's up to the scriptwriter; he or she is the one who plays God, deciding for a variety of dramatic reasons who lives or dies. The scriptwriter might write a close-up: Slowly the dismembered hand moves and rejoins its wrist. The tendons, muscles, and, finally, the skin are miraculously healed and the hand and arm look as they used to be.

**ALERT!**

The axiom in the movie business is that scripts are not written, they are rewritten. In the process, each page that is rewritten is given a new color. There have been occasions when a completed script arrived without a single white page in it.

Then the scriptwriter will save that text and go to lunch. Months later, a special effects computer technician will spend hours creating the effect that eventually audiences will gasp at. That's what the business of movie writing is all about.

# No Script—No Movie

It should be firmly fixed in the mind of every scriptwriter that even the most prestigious director would produce a mindless morass of a picture without a script. When all the actors, directors, cinematographers, and editors get up at the Oscar podium to give their thanks for their awards, they might thank the scriptwriter, without whom they wouldn't be at the podium—let alone employed—in the first place.

## The Best Screenplays over the Years

Without a screenplay there is no film, and it follows that the chance of creating a successful film is enhanced by kicking off with a good screenplay. Here is a list of well-made screenplays that served as a foundation to well-made movies. Note that most of these films demonstrated strong elements of originality.

- *Casablanca* (1942) by Julius and Philip Epstein and Howard Koch
- *Citizen Kane* (1941) by Herman Mankiewicz and Orson Welles
- *High Noon* (1952) by Carl Foreman
- *Rashomon* (1950) by Akira Kurosawa

- *The Maltese Falcon* (1941) by John Huston
- *Some Like It Hot* (1959) by Billy Wilder and I.A.L. Diamond
- *Lawrence of Arabia* (1962) by Robert Bolt

It may be interesting to note that four of these films were directed by the screenwriter: *Citizen Kane, Rashomon, The Maltese Falcon,* and *Some Like It Hot.*

## No Guarantee for Success

Unfortunately, it doesn't follow that a fine screenplay is all that's needed. Without naming names, there have been examples of films with great scripts, phenomenal casts, plus award-winning directors, cinematographers, and editors that have bombed not only with the critics but at the box office. On the other hand, there have been pictures that started off looking as if they would be a disaster on all fronts but turned out to be classic successes.

**ESSENTIAL**

To analyze a film, try to be objective and don't look at it for enjoyment alone. As a step in the right direction of trying to find out what makes a successful movie, it is suggested that readers take another look at *Double Indemnity* (1944). The screenplay is by Raymond Chandler and Billy Wilder. Pay special attention to the film's superb dialogue.

# The Screenwriter's Collaborators

It should not come as news to anyone that a film is rarely the product of one person. Just pay a quick visit to a film set, and you'll see how many people it takes just to work on the shooting. It isn't always easy for a creative individual to work as part of a team. Have you ever heard of an artist who shared the credit for his painting with others? No great painting was ever made by a team. Even in literature, few writers collaborate on novels and even fewer cowrite poems. But for the screenwriter, the reality is that her idea and creation will have to be shared and worked on by dozens—or even hundreds—of people.

## Collaborative Effort

In the ideal situation, the film production team relies on the script written by one screenwriter, and makes minimal changes to the screenwriter's vision of the film. However, in many instances this isn't the case at all. Sometimes, it's hard to say where parts of the movie came from. Consider the problem of writing a good ending.

Did you know that the ending of *American Beauty* was redone after it was viewed by a focus group? In fact, many movies have endings that weren't in the screenplay at all. Probably the most famous case of a "Who came up with the ending?" mystery in film history is the ending of *Casablanca*. As you probably remember, Ilsa goes off on the plane to Lisbon with her husband, Victor Laszlo. Rick shoots Major Strasser, then Rick and Captain Renault watch the plane as it leaves; then they go off into the fog with the famous last line from Rick: "Louis, I think this is the beginning of a beautiful friendship." But who came up with that ending?

FACT

The production manager is a key person on the set. He or she is the producer's representative and is the behind-the-scenes team player who is in charge of running the show. In most cases, the production manager is responsible for authorizing payments and paychecks.

*Casablanca* was written by the Epstein twins and Howard Koch. Apparently, it was more or less written on the fly, which often meant it went from the typewriter to the set. It's a Hollywood legend that an ending hadn't been decided on until right up to the last days of shooting. Even then, three or more versions were written and shot until the filmmakers made their final decision.

The possible candidates for writing that final ending were the Epstein twins, Howard Koch, and Casey Robinson, who collaborated in one way or another in writing the screenplay; Michael Curtiz, who directed the film; and Hal B. Wallis, the film's producer. In spite of all the excellent books on the making of *Casablanca,* the closest one can get to the truth is that the last line was an off-the-cuff last thought from producer Wallis. But even that can't be verified.

The scriptwriter should enter the fray recognizing that he or she is a member of the team and won't always be the last authority on making decisions. Sometimes, the director or the producer will decide to change the ending, the actors may choose to say their lines differently than how you had intended, and the cinematographer may prefer different shots than the ones specified in the script. This lack of control is something the screenwriter should be prepared to accept as part of the filmmaking process.

## The Shooting Script, or Scenario

So, is what you sit down to write exactly what gets distributed on the set? Not really. You write a screenplay and you send it to an agent or producer for consideration. If the screenplay is accepted and plans are made to shoot the film, your screenplay will be modified into a shooting script, or scenario. By the time a director and actors see the screenplay, it is in the form of a shooting script.

The shooting script retains all of the information included in the screenplay, but it goes into much greater detail. In other words, the shooting script has all the dialogue and description *plus* extensive technical notes like various camera directions.

The producer needs a shooting script to draw up a working budget for the production, including the costs of actors for starring roles, other characters, bit speaking parts, and extras.

Most often, the director or director's assistant will include the directions, like CUT, C.U., PAN, ZOOM, and so on. Beginning writers love to insert those directions into their screenplay, thinking that it makes the screenplay look more professional, but it actually creates the opposite impression. Unless you are specifically writing a shooting script, leave the detailed directions alone.

Most shooting scripts have the scenes numbered and rearranged in the order in which they will be shot—not necessarily the order of how the movie will be put together. So, if you need to film two scenes at the same location that are supposed to take place six months apart, they may appear together in the shooting script. For example, let's say at the beginning of the movie the hero is standing outside the Law Courts in London, waiting for a woman. Six months later, he's back at the same location, this time with a different woman. In spite of the time difference, those two scenes would be numbered sequentially and would be shot one after the other.

# The Problem of Plagiarism

Before you set out to write your screenplay, it is important to be aware of plagiarism and copyright issues. On the one hand, you need to make sure that you don't unknowingly plagiarize the work or ideas of other people. And, on the flipside, you need to protect your own material from misuse by others.

Plagiarism is the unlawful use of someone else's written work for profit. Accusations of plagiarism are not uncommon, though not that many are backed up with any evidence. Part of the problem is that the potential for plagiarism is in the system.

## Avoid Breaking the Law

It is legitimate to be influenced by the work of other artists; for instance, many writers consider themselves students of great moviemakers like Orson Welles. However, there is a gray line between being influenced by the work of another artist and deliberately copying her or his work. If you find you are being strongly influenced by the screenplay of another writer, be sure you don't cross that line into plagiarism. If you copy scenes or even lines of dialogue verbatim, you will be caught and the consequences will be severe.

**ALERT!**

Take heed of the copyright law, which says that ideas are copyrightable only when they are expressed in concrete form. However, plagiarism of another work can extend to an idea that is expressed in the concrete form of an outline and a proposal. (If in doubt, get qualified legal advice.)

## Be Aware of Your Rights

If you aren't careful, your own work may be in danger as well. There's no reason to be paranoid, just prudent. If you don't want your ideas stolen, don't send your work to just anybody, and be aware of copyright laws (see the following section). If someone in the industry asks you to show them your work, establish that person's credentials before sending out your screenplay; those who are honest will absolutely understand you making inquiries. If you don't share your ideas with anyone, it'll be difficult to get around the industry. The only option would be for you to enter into a confidentiality agreement with a potential movie buyer. To do this, you will need the assistance of a film agent or a lawyer.

If you are the average person, you will start feeling pangs of anxiety once you have sent out your pitch package, let alone a copy of your screenplay. It might help you to know that if someone does steal your property, and you can prove it's yours, you will probably make more money from a plagiarism suit than from the sale of your first spec script. However, it's doubtful if that would ever happen; for all that is said, not everyone in Hollywood is a crook.

## If You're a Victim of Plagiarism

If you do believe that someone has stolen your work, try to keep the paranoia at bay. Before you start suing people, you must establish three elements: One, that the work is not in the public domain; two, that the potential defendant had access to the material; and three, that the product sold by the defendant has sufficient similarity to your work that it can be determined that it was lifted from your work. You can start gathering your data to see if you can establish the first and second elements. The third element is the most difficult, even if one and two are cast iron. It's the part a jury would have to decide on.

# Copyrighting Your Work

Your screenplay is your property and it can be stolen, so it's important that you protect your work. Copyrighting what you write is part of every writer's job, and it is particularly important if you write screenplays. If you have an agent, he or she is responsible for registering your copyright. But if you are on your own, you will need to make sure that your work is copyrighted.

**FACT**

The famous humorist Art Buchwald sent a story outline he had written to Paramount Studios about an African prince who comes to America to find a bride. The written story was copyrighted, but the idea wasn't. Paramount decided to take the idea and make its own movie, *Coming to America,* without giving Buchwald credit. As a result, Buchwald sued Paramount for breach of agreement and won.

Remember Carl Jung's theory of the collective unconscious? Jung believed that we all share certain basic ideas and concepts. If you agree with Jung, it's not hard to see how two or more people can independently arrive at the same idea. That is why ideas cannot be owned, and you cannot copyright them. Only when they are expressed in concrete form (for example, typed in a script) can the work be copyrighted.

## The Copyright Office

If your work was produced after January 1, 1978, it is automatically copyrighted, and you will retain the rights to this work for seventy years. However, the trick is proving that it is yours. That's why there is no substitute for registration with the Copyright Office. To register copyright, all you need to do is mail them an application along with your work and registration payment. To get the application, contact the Forms and Publications Office, Library of Congress, 101 Independence Avenue SE, Washington, DC 20559-6000. You can also order copyright forms by phone at ✆ (202) 707-9100 or download them from their Web site at ✑ *http://lcweb.loc.gov/copyright*. The Web site also offers additional copyright information, which you can also receive by calling ✆ (202) 707-3000. It will take around four to six weeks to get a response. When you do, the registration is effective, even though you will not receive your certificate of registration for at least eight months.

For additional protection, screenwriters may want to send a copy of their work to the Writers Guild of America (WGA). The Guild will register your script, treatment, synopsis, or outline for five years, renewable for an additional five years. (For more information about the Writers Guild of America, see Chapter 18.)

## Losing Your Copyright

If you're lucky, however, you won't retain your copyright for very long. The surprise here is that you don't want the copyright ownership of your spec screenplay—you want to sell it to a film company. Once you sell your screenplay to a production company or studio, the copyright is transferred to whoever buys it. The screenwriter never owns the copyright of a motion picture or television movie.

**ALERT!**

Advice to the uninitiated: Don't bandy your great movie ideas about, and be sure that they are fully expressed and copyrighted before you send them to someone.

Still, as you submit your spec screenplay to studio executives, agents, and other industry insiders, you'll be reassured to know that you have already registered the copyright of your work. Remember, buying the screenplay rights is much cheaper than going through a copyright lawsuit, so very few companies will try and steal your work. Ⓔ

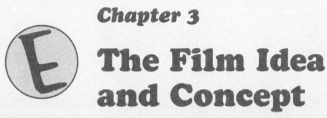

## Chapter 3

# The Film Idea and Concept

Before you start any written endeavor, whether it's a screenplay, a novel, or a short story, it's a good idea to get your intent firmly fixed in your mind. What is it you want to accomplish? Do you want to write a box-office hit and win an Oscar? To begin, you need to come up with an original idea and a clear concept of the movie that will help you achieve your goals.

# Getting Ideas

What specifically makes a movie, or gets it off the ground? The answer is almost too simple to believe: an original idea. Another way of saying idea in the business is *concept*. You are going to hear those two words and the Hollywood meaning behind them time and time again. Remember them, they're important.

Before you start writing a screenplay, it's a good idea to know what it's going to be about. How do you come up with an idea worthy of transforming into a movie? Maybe it just happens. Ever heard the phrase that the best ideas can come in the shower?

Believe it or not, it may be true for you, or an idea may dawn on you while you are out fishing, driving, watching a movie, or doing any other activity that isn't at all related to writing or consciously thinking about writing. Sometimes, the key is to stop thinking hard and let the ideas come to you.

What you will be searching for is the elusive story that Sam Goldwyn talked about: "A great picture has to start with a great story. The bigger the stars, the director, and producer, the harder they fall on a bad story."

Intuition, which in this context is another word for inspiration, can play a great role in creation. Learn to trust your gut feeling. The more you trust it, the stronger it will tend to become.

## Finding Inspiration

All writers of any merit should look at human nature, both historically and currently, and absorb from it as it suits his or her creativity. So, remember that right from the beginning of the creative process we are heavily involved in the subjective—subjective not only in terms of opinion about our own work and the work of others, but in our selections as they are exhibited in the choice of what we want to use, either directly or indirectly. Never forget that you will write as you are.

What you pick to write in your script will, particularly at the beginning of your writing career, come from your subjective viewpoint. The great writer Willa Cather wrote, "In the beginning, the artist, like his public, is wedded to old forms, old ideals, and his vision is blurred by the memory of old delights he would like to recapture." The writer should operate from an open mind, one that is capable of seeing all points of view. Learn, therefore, to distinguish the subject from the object.

**FACT**

Here's what the writer Alberto Moravia had to say about writing: "When I sit at my table to write, I never know what it's going to be until I'm underway. I trust inspiration, which sometimes comes and sometimes doesn't. But I don't sit back waiting for it. I work every day."

## Keeping Your Audience in Mind

As you think about your film idea, you need to envision whom it is you will be writing for. Think about your target audience and what their experiences and expectations may be.

When the audience gets comfortable in a cinema, all ready to see the new Julia Roberts film, for instance, it is a reasonable assumption that they are aware of what they're in for. Invariably, there have been pages and pages of advertising and reviews of the picture to prime them. In addition, they are fans of Ms. Roberts and she rarely lets them down. In exactly the same way, an audience knows how films move along; whether they are informed about film production or not, they know there will be a beginning, a middle, and an end (most prefer happy endings).

**ALERT!**

Sometimes writers become overly involved in creating a film related to a current event or trendy topic. They get so tied up in it being contemporary that they forget that even if it were bought right now, it would take at least a year or more to get to the cinemas. By then the chances are that "timely" would have lost its attraction.

## Knowing What It Takes

If you'd like to write a screenplay that has a chance of becoming an instant hit with the audience, it may be useful to take a look at some of the top-grossing domestic blockbusters. They can tell you more than just the fact that *Titanic* is the top-grossing movie of all time at $600.8 million in domestic revenue. According to the MovieWeb site, the following are the top ten as of 2002, in descending order:

1. *Titanic*
2. *Star Wars*
3. *E.T. the Extra-Terrestrial*
4. *Star Wars: Episode 1, The Phantom Menace*
5. *Spider-Man*
6. *Jurassic Park*
7. *Forrest Gump*
8. *The Lion King*
9. *Harry Potter and the Sorcerer's Stone*
10. *The Lord of the Rings: The Two Towers*

A quick look at the titles will tell you that all ten films fall into the family fare category. Take another look and you'll see that interestingly, so far this century, three of the films to reach the top ten in gross revenues were based on previously written material: *Spider-Man*, *The Lord of the Rings*, and *Harry Potter*. Of the others, six were original screenplays as well as being science fiction or fantasy.

Incidentally, Aristotle was the man who introduced the concept of the three-act play (first act introduces the plot and characters, second act develops the characters and builds up suspense, and third act leads to resolution). This remains the basic structure of most screenplays today.

# Choosing a Film Genre

Movies, like books, are slotted into categories or genres. We attribute the concept of genres in literature to the Greek philosopher Aristotle, the author of *Poetics*. Although it was written many centuries ago, *Poetics* has had great influence over the development of Western literature and the way we categorize it. *Poetics* is actually about writing for the theater, which was invented by the ancient Greeks. In *Poetics*, Aristotle theorizes that all theater productions may be divided into tragedy, comedy, and epic.

**FACT**

They say the Western is dead. But Hollywood tends to be cyclical, so you never know. The writer/director most recognized as the last Western creator of merit is Sergio Leone of *The Good, the Bad, and the Ugly* fame. His finest production is said to have been *Once Upon a Time in the West* with Henry Fonda as a sadistic killer and Jason Robards, Claudia Cardinale, and Charles Bronson.

The movie industry has many more genres as well as subgenres. The basic film genres are:

- Action/adventure: *Anaconda*, the Indiana Jones series
- Comedy: *Some Like It Hot, Dumb and Dumber*
- Crime: *The Godfather* movies, *Ocean's Eleven*
- Drama: *Taxi Driver, Rain Man*
- Epic: *Ben-Hur, Titanic*
- Horror: *The Exorcist, Nightmare on Elm Street*
- Juvenile: *Willy Wonka and the Chocolate Factory, Stuart Little*
- Musical: *Moulin Rouge, Chicago*
- Science fiction: *Total Recall, Blade Runner*
- War: *Platoon, Saving Private Ryan*
- Western: *The Great Train Robbery, Billy the Kid*

## Choosing Your Genre

It's a good idea to decide where to sow your idea. That is, you should establish at the beginning what genre you're going to work with. What might work well in a comedy could ruin a drama. When thinking about a category, think of what is appropriate for it—even matters like a typical budget will make a difference. Obviously, an action film generally requires a bigger budget than a comedy.

To help you get creative with choosing a genre, think of subgenres. For example, what is the subgenre of *Butch Cassidy and the Sundance Kid*, any of *The Lethal Weapon* pictures, and *Thelma and Louise*? They are all "buddy" movies. Or, think of a subgenre and then list the first three films that come to mind—that will help you figure out which films fit best into a particular category.

**QUESTION?**

**Do styles or types of films change over the years?**
Yes and no. Westerns, which used to be a staple of Hollywood production, are now quite rare. Action adventures backed by an array of special effects have become the new Westerns. It's like what they say about the fashion business—there's nothing new in fashion except fancy dress.

## The Film Noir

Once you pick a genre, investigate it further—try to figure out what film was the first of its kind and how the history of that genre developed. Let's take the example of film noir. The genre emerged after World War II and featured films that were dark mystery stories. A strong element of the film noir genre has always been cynicism; generally, film noir themes are downbeat and film noir characters are brooding, dark personalities with an undercurrent of moral dignity under a hard shell.

The film noir genre was fueled by a group of writers, among the best known of whom were the following.

- Raymond Chandler: *Farewell, My Lovely; The Long Goodbye*
- Graham Greene: *This Gun for Hire; Brighton Rock*
- Dashiell Hammett: *The Maltese Falcon; The Dain Curse*
- Chester Himes: *Blind Man with a Pistol; The Crazy Kill*
- Gerald Kersh: *Night and the City*
- Cornell Woolrich: *The Bride Wore Black; Rendezvous in Black*

# Write about Your Interests

Most writers find out early on in their careers that they have a feeling for a certain kind of story. Try to follow the principle that what you love doing, you do well, because it will probably lead you in the right direction. If you absolutely love action books and action films, then maybe that's what you should write. If you are a mystery fan, maybe a film noir is the thing for you. If you're interested in historical romances, why not use what you already know to write a screenplay?

As we all know, everything has been done before, but not your way. The way you write will be a reflection of who you are, everything that you are. The sum of that will become the basis of your style. The most important element is that you have strong feelings for the subject matter you intend writing about. In fact, anger isn't a bad motivator.

## Time and Place

Once you've pinpointed your interest, also consider the timing and place of the story. These factors can have tremendous influence, mainly on the sales potential of the screenplay. If a budding screenwriter has become obsessed with figures of historical significance, for instance, some lower-class, little-known fellow who led a devastating charge on the British troops in one of their former colonies, he or she will have a more than a difficult job convincing a studio to even take a look at the outline.

The leading reason for rejecting such a project would be the thought of its budget. Historical subjects are not popular with the film industry anymore. Just imagine the cost of all those costumes, to say nothing of the locations with their castles, drawbridges, and horses.

It is a truism that if a studio can find a good reason for rejecting a screenplay, they'll find one. This is because of the vast number they receive. Thus, it becomes prudent for screenwriters to choose their subject matter wisely. The possible cost of the project should be a major consideration.

It can take from $1 million to $130 million to develop a film script from scratch to a finished product in the cinemas. It's no small wonder, therefore, that with that kind of money at risk producers can get a shade picky when a new script from an unknown writer arrives.

## The Inner Purpose of a Screenplay

It doesn't matter which of the suggested ideas/concepts you pick to work from; there is usually more to the finished screenplay product than just a wide-ranging category title. In all matters of written creativity there is at the base of the endeavor the need to comment on the human condition.

This doesn't mean that you all of a sudden have to become a new-age scriptwriter. Two people falling in love and then falling out of love, how that happens and how they deal with the problem—that's part of the human condition just as much as any situation might be. The scriptwriter creates characters and allows the fates to throw them together, just like in real life.

## Research Your Domain

If you want to be a successful screenwriter, you have to immerse yourself in movies, learning everything you can about the way they are written and made. Quentin Tarantino, the director of *Reservoir Dogs* and *Pulp Fiction*, which in 1994 won him an Oscar for best original screenplay, did his research by working in a video rental store. The influence from the videos he must have seen can be identified in his work. For instance, *Reservoir Dogs* draws inspiration from Stanley

Kubrick's *The Killing* and Martin Scorsese's *Mean Streets,* among others. An even more successful director, Steven Spielberg, spent his formative years directing TV's *Marcus Welby, M.D.*, and *Columbo* instead of going to college, learning by experience.

Many screenwriters also begin their careers in film school, where they have an opportunity to write screenplays for budding directors. Those who form working relationships with directors may later have the opportunity to write for them in Hollywood. If you are really interested in getting formal training in screenwriting, the best source of information regarding accredited film schools is probably the Library of Annotated Film Schools (LOAFS). There is a book in preparation by graduates from NYU called *Film School Confidential.* In the meanwhile, LOAFS provides a comprehensive listing of film schools around the world (✑ *http://filmmaker.com/loafs*).

# The Concept

Once you've got your idea, you'll need to flesh it out into a concept, which is basically a fancy word that refers to a film idea description that will help you sell the screenplay. In fact, revved-up writers determined to sell their idea go a step further and call it "high concept."

## The "Meets" Line

One of the best approaches to creating a concept is to do it with the "meets" line, a log line and pitch hook that includes the word "meets." The "meets" line can help you instantly accomplish, capture, and convey in just a single line of words the concept (idea) of the proposed film.

**ALERT!**

As you come up with your "meets" line, don't forget to keep the budget in mind. Mentioning films like *Titanic* will send a message that your idea is going to require a costly production. Unless you believe that you've got a winning concept, it's always a plus to pitch a script that isn't going to cost millions to produce.

On the face of it, a hook or "meets" line may seem pretty silly, even for Hollywood. However, surprisingly they can sum up, by presenting a mental image that is already in the mind of the reader, just what the film is about. Let's say a screenwriter tells you that his new idea is *Calamity Jane* meets *King Kong*. From that simple phrase, you'll get a good feel for what the concept of the screenplay is—you'll probably get an instant image of dear Doris Day in her cowgirl outfit with a stuffed gorilla on top of the Empire State Building. (If you don't want to sound too dated, you may want to pick more recent films for your "meets" line.)

## Film Length

As you continue working on your concept, it may be useful for you to know the length of an average feature-length film. The average film today is somewhere around 120 minutes long. The reason most films are 90 to 120 minutes long is very simple: People have to sit still in order to watch, and in our day and age most people don't have a long attention span. If you make the movie too long, your audience may lose interest. Another reason is economics—the longer the film, the more money you will need to produce it. Furthermore, the length of the film dictates how many times it can be shown in the cinema during the time it's open. If it's very long, the exhibitor will lose the income from at least one screening each day. (Unless the price of the seats is increased for that film—not a popular marketing idea.)

Motion pictures in the past have been hours long, but not anymore. Today, your audience will come to the movie theater, settle in with their food and drinks, and will generally watch for the next hour and a half or so (few people ever walk out of a movie). However, if the movie is long, you may run the risk of losing your audience.

## Give Your Creation a Name

To paraphrase Raymond Chandler: A good title is the title of a successful film. Ideally, a title should evoke in the mind of the reader a shiver of excitement. A good title is unforgettable and provides clues to what the film is about and what genre it belongs to. It's a plus if your title raises a direct or implied question, because questions need answers and thereby involve the audience and pique their attention.

It is unlikely that you will sit down at a keyboard and channel a brilliant title, like Orson Welles's *Touch of Evil.* But at some point, a good title may suddenly pop into your mind. The key is to write it down immediately—even if you don't think it's that great. Most writers get into the habit of carrying a small notebook for such occasions. What happens when you don't have a notebook is that you rush around trying to find a piece of paper and something to write with because you know from experience that unless you write down the scintillating words, they will vanish into memory hell.

**FACT**

In the early days of film, it was more common than it is today for Hollywood to hire novelists to come to the West Coast to write film scripts. F. Scott Fitzgerald, Dorothy Parker, Nathanael West, Mario Puzo, Aldous Huxley, Truman Capote, and William Faulkner all wrote for Hollywood.

There are many titles that, before the film they heralded became famous, didn't really mean very much—think of films like *Rocky, Serpico, Casablanca, Citizen Kane.* Other famous titles bring with them the glory of the books that have paved the way for the films on which they're based, like *Gone with the Wind, The Wizard of Oz, The Grapes of Wrath,* and *Frankenstein.* (An association with something already known, and sometimes loved, by the reader/viewer tends to be a presell.)

## Chapter 4

# Writing the Treatment and Synopsis

After you've got the idea and concept figured out, the next step in the creative process of writing a screenplay is to create a treatment and synopsis. The treatment is a detailed outline written in present tense. A synopsis goes into even more detail, outlining the film scene by scene.

# Introduction to the Treatment

A treatment is a means of telling the story of the proposed screenplay. Treatments don't need to go into great detail, so there is no need to spell out each scene individually. A good treatment needs to tell the overall story of the film quickly and concisely.

A treatment can serve several purposes. First of all, writing a treatment will allow you to solidify your idea and will give you a more detailed plan that you'll be able to rely on as you begin to write the screenplay. Secondly, you can use your treatment to try and sell your film idea to an agent or producer, either by sending it to them or by using it as you make a verbal pitch over the telephone or at a meeting.

## QUESTION?

**How long should a treatment be?**
There's no assigned length, but avoid overwriting. Put yourself in the place of an average agent or producer. Most of them are busy people. It's unlikely they'll want to bother with reading anything that's more than a few pages long.

Many professional scriptwriters hate writing treatments, but it's an important part of beginning the process of writing, and you shouldn't skip it. Think of it this way: The treatment is the blueprint for your screenplay. Without it, you risk running into major problems as you work on your screenplay.

Until you have a track record, it's very unlikely that you will sell a screenplay without first having a treatment to show. However, having a treatment but no screenplay isn't a good idea either. If a producer becomes interested in your idea while you still don't have the screenplay ready, you may have to sell your idea to be written by other screenwriters.

## Know Who You're Writing For

As you begin your treatment, keep in mind your audience—this isn't your average moviegoer, but the agent or producer reading your treatment. Although you may not think it, knowing whom you are writing for gives you an element of power. You are the wielder of the words and it is the words that are going to influence the reader, so choose them carefully.

**ALERT!**

The way your work is prepared and submitted is very important. The material should give the impression of professionalism and that means no spelling or gross grammatical errors. It should look as if you know what you're doing. Even though the content of your work is what will sell it, the way it's presented is vital.

Keep in mind that your target audience is the decision makers who receive such treatments in great numbers every week. What, you might ask, is going to set yours off from all the others? Excellence might be a good guess, because, fortunately, a lot of what these people receive is terrible stuff. It's a truth that most of the competition is no competition at all; they just get in the way. Your real competitors are the writers who are already doing very nicely writing screenplays that get produced.

Look in any of the reference books relating to agents and you'll see that they all say that they reject about 98 percent of everything they receive. You, dear reader, would reject at least 50 percent of everything an agent receives, including the handwritten stuff scribbled on napkins or adhesive notes, and your experience of the business is not that extensive. So, as long as you have a good, original idea presented in a clear and reasonable fashion, you've got a real chance to get the attention you are looking for.

## Third Person, Present Tense

The treatment should always be written in the third person (he/she/they) and in the present tense (now)—the advantage of writing in the present tense is its immediacy. Generally, you should avoid including direct dialogue in your treatment.

Not everybody is adept at writing in the present tense. This is mainly because most of us are used to writing in the past tense. The past tense comes easily to us all, and we've been using it for most of our lives. Using the present tense is a conscious literary device.

To help yourself become more comfortable with using the present tense, always keep in mind that you are writing for the movies and what the audience sees on the screen is what happens in front of the camera. Even if the scene takes place in the eighteenth century, the scene is being shot in the present. That's how it will be written in the script, and that is how treatments and synopses should be written. The form is ingrained in the business and everyone in it accepts the written present tense without second thought.

**FACT**

Although literary ability is not a required talent for screenplays, it is for treatments, which is one reason, perhaps, that many scriptwriters don't like writing them. Most people short on writing talent, or new to it, overwrite. It is essential that treatments are well-paced, clear, and easy to read.

Here's how you would use third person/present tense writing in the mode of a treatment to describe what happens in *Fargo:*

A car salesman in a Minnesota backwater hires a couple of lowlifes to kidnap his wife so that his wealthy father-in-law will pay a ransom big enough to get him out of trouble. They pull it off, but during a drive in the snow at night they just happen to commit three murders. The bright police chief, who is very pregnant and speaks in a slow sort of Norwegian-type accent, investigates . . .

## Avoid Author Intrusion

There's something in narrative prose called *author intrusion.* It happens when the author gets into the act and starts being a nuisance, either by overexplaining or by telling the readers how they should feel. Even best-selling authors do it. However, in a treatment it's an absolute no-no.

Here are a few examples of the "author intrusion" type of writing that might be seen in poor character thumbnail sketches:

- The hero is this fantastic stud.
- He makes an amazing jump you wouldn't believe.
- The heroine was abused by her father.
- She's a closet lesbian.

If your treatment sounds like that, it's not unlikely that you'll get a quick rejection—no explanation needed. The author should never be present in the narrative, so always stay out of sight. Show, don't tell.

It is always better not to tell the reader how characters feel; if you describe the actions of the characters, the reader will understand without being told. For instance, let's say that at the beginning of the film, your protagonist accidentally runs over a pedestrian, and is so agitated by the experience that she freaks out and drives away without thinking of the consequences. In your treatment, you don't need to go into great detail describing how this character feels. All you need to write is something like: "As she turns the corner, Sarah hits a pedestrian. When she realizes what has happened, she gets back in and speeds away."

**ESSENTIAL**

You can practice how you might write treatments by going over in your mind what a film you just saw was about. The interesting thing about doing this is that often the film was so weak you can't remember what it was about in any detail. Make sure that isn't the case with your treatment, let alone your script.

## A Treatment of *Loophole*

The best way to learn how to write a great treatment is to look at a detailed example. Here we've got the treatment of my novel *Loophole*, which I had rewritten as a screenplay for the film produced in 1980. Take heed of the technical details here to be sure that your treatment has a professional polish to it.

**LOOPHOLE**

**A Treatment**

**Robert Pollock**


**The Bank That Couldn't Be Robbed**


Robert Pollock

ADDRESS

PHONE NUMBER

**Cockney Mike Daniels**, an ace thief and master safe-cracker, has a major, fail-safe plan: how to crack an uncrackable vault in an unrobbable London bank and get away with millions.

He finds **Stephen Booker,** an out-of-work architect and civil engineer, whose comfortable suburban life is coming apart, including his marriage. Daniels picks his brains, wears down his moral resistance, and hires him.

Then he puts together a band of five expert thieves, and lays out his plan: to go down into the London sewers under the bank, negotiate the black, rat-infested waters, and tunnel up into the vault.

**Stephen Booker** demonstrates his expert contribution to the plan, which is superbly detailed.

They have one weekend to do the job. The vault door has a time lock. It won't function until the opening of business Monday morning. In that time frame the group has to dig a tunnel under the vault, bore up into the floor of the vault, and blast open a way in.

There is the constant danger of lethal gas in the tunnel. **Booker** discovers that Daniels has concealed diving equipment stashed; if it rains outside on the London streets, the sewers will flood.

The alarms sound, the police arrive. As there is no

sign above in the bank of a forced entry, they mount a surveillance and wait. Down inside the vault the robbery goes on. The rains come and the tunnel starts to flood.

**Booker** decides to stay and risk the flood; the water is slowly rising to the top of the tunnel. **Daniels** puts his diving equipment on. The others in the sewer are frantically swimming away in an effort to get to a way out and climb up to a manhole cover at street level.

At a sewage pumping station down from the bank, a screen filter stops large pieces of debris from fouling up the works. A technician inspects the filter screen. He sees the matted head of a man floating in the sewage. (There is a time transition.)

A moving van at the driveway to a suburban house is being loaded. A woman, **Stephen Booker's wife**, sees the postman coming up the drive. She goes to meet him and takes the mail. She looks through the mail and studies a postcard of a beach. She calls into the house: Darling, who do we know in Australia?

ENDS.

## The Cover

We are always told not to judge a book by its cover, but we do anyway, so it's important to do a good job on your treatment cover page. At the center, write the title of the film you propose. Next line is reserved for the words "A Treatment." And underneath that you should include your full name.

Next, include a one-sentence log line that describes the film, designed mainly to create anticipation in the reader. In the case of *Loophole*, the log line is "The Bank That Couldn't Be Robbed." Down at the bottom left of the page, you can type in your personal details; if you have an agent, leave it blank—the agent will fill it in.

## The Main Text

There are all sorts of opinions about how a treatment should look. Forget any frills or tricky stuff: no colored paper or odd-looking fonts. Take an absolutely businesslike approach. Use 12-point Courier font, make sure your margins are set at 1 inch away from the edge, and set the text double-spaced, with indents to indicate paragraphs.

Some writers adopt a technique used by newspapers in their celebrity columns. They put the names of the celebrities in bold type. That way the reader can scan the names until he or she gets to one of personal interest. Some treatment writers put plot points, character names, tone, story progression, and such in bold type. The idea here is that the very busy reader can skip the details and just pick up the gist.

## The Necessary Elements

After reading the treatment of *Loophole,* what kind of information do you have? As you can see, this treatment conveys what the film is all about—it's a caper movie, full of danger and suspense. There are the suggested names of the lead characters, with brief descriptions of each one; the detailed plan and how it gets derailed; and the conclusion. Essentially, this treatment contains the bare three-act form the script will take: the setup, what goes wrong, and the resolution.

# Now It's Time to Write Your Own

So, you've got your idea and maybe even the cover page of the treatment. Now it's time to start writing. Your first draft should contain a basic overview of the film—the events in the order that they will appear in the film (which is not necessarily the chronological order) and enough information to get a sense about the film's main characters. Once you've got something tangible, it's time to get a second opinion.

**FACT**

The three-act form has lasted because it's based on life. The first act is from birth to the end of the teenage years. It is the act full of introduction and discovery. The second act, the longest, is the toughest one in life as well as in a screenplay. The third act is the act of resolution, and it always has the same ending.

## Getting Critical Advice

Run off a few copies of the treatment and show them around to your relatives and friends. Just tell them it's an outline for a movie idea and ask them to let you know what they think. It's best not to prompt the readers with casual phrases like, "Just let me know if you think it has any tension." It will bias your friends and allow those who don't want to hurt you to give you the answer you more or less asked for.

It's always difficult trying to figure out if the opinions you get are worth anything. Do your friends know anything about the film business? Are they frequent moviegoers? Are they eager to support your film aspirations or, on the contrary, looking for a way to bring you down? Try to get past these biases and see what they really think. What you are looking for is interest in your idea. If you ask for their thoughts and they tell you that it was "interesting," what they're really saying is that it's nothing too special. If, on the other hand, you hear something like, "It was fantastic, I mean, cool, man!" you've really got their attention, so you're definitely in business.

Most importantly, pay attention to specific details that your friends mention after reading your treatment. Try to see which details were more memorable and effective, and which parts evoked confusion—those you'll need to change. Also try finding out how your friends envisioned the characters—if their impression matches what you had in mind, you're off to a very good start.

**ALERT!**

No matter how people react to your work, keep in mind that this is your first draft and that you can change it any way you want—rewrite the ending, add or get rid of characters, or even change the setting.

## Going Back to Your Desk

When you've got the feedback and advice of several people, it's time to go back to your treatment and begin the rewriting process. Though it may be a tedious task, it is in your best interest to stick with it until you've got a treatment that exactly expresses your idea for the film in clear and precise language that draws the reader in and doesn't let go until the end. Once you're done with the treatment, you can go on to expand it into a synopsis.

## Writing a Synopsis

A synopsis is a detailed outline of the film. Be prepared to invest a fair amount of time and energy in the composition of yours. You will find it is a tremendous drawback to any presentation, written or made in person, if your outline/synopsis sounds flat; enthusiasm is essential. As Ralph Waldo Emerson said, "Nothing great was ever achieved without enthusiasm."

The simplest way to write a synopsis, after you've written a treatment, is to follow the treatment's form but flesh it all out. A detailed synopsis may be as long as thirty pages, so when you start writing the screenplay, you won't have to begin from scratch.

The format of a synopsis cover page should duplicate the cover page of the treatment (see Appendix C), with two exceptions: Obviously, you'll write "A Synopsis" instead of "A Treatment"; secondly, you should use Times Roman as the font and pick whichever point size you think works best. The body text of the synopsis should be 12-point Times Roman, double-spaced, with page numbering.

**Should I write a synopsis as well as a treatment?**
A straight answer is difficult to give because different situations call for different actions. It certainly won't do any harm and it will definitely help you when you write the screenplay. If you're asked to do one, then, of course, do it.

## Let's Take a Look at Our Example

To take *Loophole* as our example, you would begin by expanding on how Booker and Daniels met and go into greater depth about Booker's married life, which obviously Daniels would use as leverage to persuade Booker to come in with him. You'll also need to add in the details of the heist plan. Then, expand on the conflict between the thieves and how it develops, how the plan is carried out, and the ending.

Now, let's presume that we begin reading the synopsis at a point in act two, when the characters are preparing for the heist and are faced with a sort of emergency. Here is an excerpt from the synopsis:

A small group of them gather around the pontoon smoking, drinking hot tea from a thermos, and resting. Mike Daniels tells them it's time they all got back to work. Harry says he'll check the lamps again; Mike tells him to be sure he does that every half-hour.

They go back to digging and dragging out the loose mud and filling the trolley so that the entrance to the sewer shaft that is nearest to them can be blocked. It is a hard, hot, tiring routine and they take it in shifts. Only Taylor doesn't help with the digging. A change has come over him; he seems to have lost his sense of command, and the others resent it.

Down the sewer shaft, Harry checks the alarm lamps hanging

on the walls of the sewer. He talks to himself to keep his spirits up. He is getting tired. His breathing is becoming labored and his legs start to drag in the sewage. He keeps shaking his head, and his eyelids are drooping as if they have lost their power to stay open. He sees the glimmer of the last alarm lamp; he staggers and clutches at the wall of the sewer. He swears, slips, and crashes into the sewage. His lamp goes under the surface of the water and light from its watertight shell sends bent, wavy liquid shafts through the water. He drags himself up, lunges forward, slips again, and bounces from wall to wall in a frenzy and panic of trying to run from something he can't see. He tries to shout out but his voice is a low gurgled croak.

Taylor is pushing a trolley along the shaft and sees the crazy swinging of the light coming at him from beyond the pontoon. Then he sees Harry, covered with sewage and grime, and the obscene mouth that is trying to spit out vomit and words. He cries out for help; his voice is a screech. Daniels comes from the upper sewer; he tries to run against the pressure of the sewer water. He sees Taylor's white face and Harry's smeared stinking features and the alarm lamp that has turned red, all at the same time. He yells out for everyone to get masks.

They tear at the containers on the pontoon and pull out the tubes, bottles, and masks that make up the oxygen equipment. They struggle to get the masks on. Harry collapses in the sewage and the rats overcome their fright and attack him. The others fight against the effects of the gas in the sewer. The rats squeak and try to scamper into the darkness, but the gas is affecting them too. The men beat at the rats with picks and chisels. There is a frenzy of splashing red water.

Taylor and Daniels pull Harry's limp body from the sewage and drag it onto the pontoon. They get an oxygen mask on him and wait. Suddenly it is calm. Daniels reaches to check Harry's pulse, then he looks up at the alarm lamps; the one farthest away is changing color from red back to a thin yellow. Then the lamp next to it changes, then another. It looks as if a ghost is moving through the sewer telling them it is all clear.

The men start to take their masks off. They sniff the air and know the danger has passed. They turn to Harry, and Taylor tears the mask from his face. The face is gray and through the slime Taylor can see the blood-red bite marks made by the rats. One of the men turns away and vomits into the sewage. Taylor seems to have regained his strength and becomes a leader again. He tells them to get the brandy and the first-aid kit.

Taylor cleans Harry's face with the brandy and cotton swabs. When his face is clean Taylor puts his mouth over Harry's and gives him the kiss of life. The others stand silently and watch. Suddenly Taylor turns and looks up. He tells them Harry is coming out of it. There are visible signs of relief from the men. Taylor does his best to cover the rat bites with gauze and make Harry comfortable. There is talk about getting Harry to a doctor as soon as they can.

The sound-powered telephone buzzes. Mike looks at the receiver and lets it buzz some more, then he picks it up. He listens and makes only perfunctory replies. He hangs up. The others wait. He tells them that the lookout said the weather forecast is for some thundershowers and that most of the staff at the bank have left for the weekend.

---

This extract has the necessary ingredients for creating tension, the sentences are short and to the point, and there is no superfluous narrative—every word has a purpose. Most importantly, and this is vital in both a treatment and a synopsis, the reader should be able to "see" the action as it happens.

Keep in mind that what you are writing here is a selling document, so make it move, give it some drama, and write it so that it's an easy read. Again, it's important that you write the synopsis in the third person, present tense.

# Chapter 5
# Screenplay Structure

The actions in your screenplay form the plot, which may be broken down into three acts. This chapter will investigate the basic three-act structure of most screenplays and how you can use it to your advantage—to have a clear beginning, middle, and end; to build suspense; and to have a meaningful resolution.

# A Basic Three-Act Breakdown

If in any doubt about why the methods used to construct a screenplay haven't changed over the years, ask yourself why every writing teacher, of either screenplays or books, always makes strong mention of that ancient Greek called Aristotle. Aristotle was born in a place called Stagira in Greece in 384 B.C.E., which places him over two thousand years back in history. In 350 B.C.E. he wrote a work called *Poetics*, which has influenced the structure of plays—and then screenplays—for hundreds of years.

**ESSENTIAL**

> "The plot, then, is the first principle, and, as it were, the soul of a tragedy; Character holds the second place . . . Thus Tragedy is the imitation of an action, and of the agents mainly with a view to the action." —Aristotle

One of Aristotle theories was that a story should be written in three acts, because every story should have a beginning, a middle, and an end. And this is true of most films today. In fact, each of the acts is allotted a specific amount of time. The first act should last about thirty minutes. This is a time when you set the scene and introduce the characters. The second act should last for about an hour, and during this time is when most of the action takes place and the suspense builds. The third act takes another thirty minutes and includes the resolution of the film—think of it as tying up all the loose ends. Because in a screenplay, one page is typically equivalent to one minute of screen time, most screenplays are roughly 120 pages long (that's counting all the dialogue, silences, and action).

Such is the insistence to form in the movie business that if you start punting a script around that is 200 pages long (and your name is not Coppola or Spielberg), you are going to make a career out of rejection. Your script should be between 90 and 120 pages long.

## The Plot, the Subplot, and the Subtext

The three acts constitute the plot, or what happens, and each "happening" is a plot point—think of plot points as turning points in the story. A subplot and subtext generally evolve from the plot to make the surface story more interesting. The purpose of a subplot is to provide new interest and add more substance to the plot, in particular to the lengthier and more eventful second act. The subtext is literally what happens underneath the text. That is, it's the thoughts and motivations never directly expressed by the characters.

**ALERT!**

Practice dividing films you see into three acts. One good film to view with the three-act structure in mind is *The Conversation,* written and directed by Francis Ford Coppola. Note that the running time is 113 minutes.

For example, let's say you write a romantic comedy with a basic three-act structure:

1. Boy meets girl.
2. Boy loses girl.
3. Boy wins girl.

The subplot may be an added story. Let's say the male protagonist has trouble at work and is falsely accused of embezzlement. The prosecutor of the case turns out to be the female protagonist's sister. The subtext here may be the sister's secret crush on the male protagonist and her internal conflict between doing a good job and being a lenient prosecutor. Because the subtext is generally comprised of the thoughts and feelings that are implied but never stated, it is difficult to write it into the script.

## The Back Story

The plot and subplot generally rely on the *back story*—what happens in a plot before the screen story begins. The back story is often conveyed by exposition, or nondialogue text. Although it's important to set the back-story elements, many writers tend to overexplain. One way to avoid exposition is by writing flashback scenes that show, rather than explain, what has actually happened in the past.

## The First Ten Minutes

It has not escaped the attention of many people that we now live in the age of the short attention span. More than ever this has produced the need, in all forms of written/visual work, to hook the consumer in a hurry. If you don't, they'll put the book back on the shelf, skip to a different radio station, switch the TV channel, or turn the magazine page. In film, the key is to draw the viewer into the movie within the first ten minutes—and some now advocate that this critical period is only five minutes long!

**FACT**

The 1967 film *Bonnie and Clyde* was a roaring success. The screenplay, written by David Newman and Robert Benton, was hardly a typical Hollywood work—in fact, it was an homage to the French New Wave films popular overseas in the 1960s.

If the film has a strong megatype star as the lead, it's important for the screenplay to allow the star to enter the screen as early as possible. The producers wouldn't want the audience to think the megastar wasn't going to show up. And the reason the star is a star is probably because he or she is able to draw in and captivate the audience.

## Not Relying on a Star

However, you don't always have to rely on a big star to make your first ten minutes work. Here's where you can learn from successes in the independent-film industry. Many of them do economically better than blockbusters, and the explanation is actually simple. While a blockbuster must spend millions of dollars on top-name actors and special effects, the independent films have a small budget and no overpriced stars to coddle. Even though they make less in box-office revenue, the bottom line is that they make more than they spend.

Here are just a handful of independent productions that are excellent examples: *Four Weddings and a Funeral*; *The Full Monty*; *Crouching Tiger, Hidden Dragon*; and *My Big Fat Greek Wedding*. Perhaps that might say something about the stories and the actors?

# The First Act

The function of the first act is very simple—to introduce the rest of the film. This may be why the first act of a screenplay is often called the *setup*. And all the introductions and back story must be filled in over a period of roughly thirty minutes (or thirty script pages).

It has been ingrained over the years that the audience needs to be nudged when an act is over and the film is moving forward into the next one. In film, this is generally done with the introduction of the first plot point.

## Plot Points

Plot points are also known as *action points, transition points,* and *turning points.* They all more or less mean the same thing, which is to indicate the end/beginning of an act by presenting a complete twist in the plot trajectory. For instance, boy meets girl, they fall in love, and everything looks lovely. Plot point: His wife shows up.

The first plot point should occur around the end of the first act and should take the script into the second act, which as we all know is the longest. The second major plot point separates the second and third acts.

Take a look at your three-act organization. The three acts should be cohesive, three parts of an organic whole that tell a story with a beginning, a middle, and an end.

There are other places, too, in a screenplay where additional (minor) plot points can be used. They would indicate change elements of a less dramatic nature. Just be sure that the two major ones that show the act changes are in their proper places.

# The Second Act

The action begins in the second act. By the time you make the transition to the second act, the audience should be completely involved in the film and most of the characters should have been introduced. The second act is the act of tension and of action, as the audience wonders how the plot will ever be resolved: Will he get the girl? Will she crack the case? Will they escape the serial killer and provide enough evidence to get him safely behind bars?

It's okay for the second act to be very eventful, as long as the plot is progressing toward some point. However, if the writer runs out of steam and starts floundering, what the audience gets is a series of disconnected events that won't achieve a sense of suspense and will lead nowhere. In that case, the audience will quickly lose interest and the film will be a flop.

**QUESTION?**

**Do I have to strictly follow the three-act format?**
No, you don't, but it would be better to wait until you are experienced before you start experimenting. The three-act format is what film people expect; if you don't give it to them, many will be thrown off-kilter.

Sometimes the problem is that too much has already been done in the first act. The characters have already been so deeply characterized that there was not much left in the way of developing them further in the second act, and they appear flat and uninteresting. Or perhaps certain characters got no attention in the first act and now that they've joined the cast in the second act, we know nothing about them. This is a major reason why a writer should devote time and energy to the screenplay outline; the forward motion should be well plotted before it's written out, all three acts of it.

## Conflict and Confrontation

The second act should set up conflicts for the characters to figure out; in fact, some people refer to the second act as "the confrontation act." Remember our example of the man who falls in love, and then his wife enters the scene? The conflict here is between the new love and the wife. Should he stay with the wife or with the new lover? Should his wife try to win him back or dump him? Should the new lover fight for this man or tell him to go back to the wife? Through the course of this act, events will move these three characters toward some kind of a resolution, to come in act three.

# The Third Act

The last half-hour of the film deals with the resolution, brought about by the major plot point that carries the plot from the second to the third act. This is the most dramatic plot point of the film, the climax of the story, which will affect how the story will be resolved.

When it comes to creating the second major plot point, there are many options for you to consider; a trip to the video store might give you some pointers. Here are two examples from the oldies.

The third act of *Casablanca* kicks off when Ilsa comes to Rick's room to demand the letters of transit at gunpoint. She can't shoot Rick. Her line of dialogue at that point is the arc of the second–third act transition: "I don't know what's right any longer. You have to decide for both of us, for all of us." The third act resolves the film as Rick makes all the decisions, and Ilsa and Laszlo leave in the airplane.

The second–third act transition arc in *Some Like It Hot* arrives when the 1920s-style gangsters arrive at the Florida hotel where the second act has played out, and one of them seems to recognize "the two broads" from the all-girl band, played by Tony Curtis and Jack Lemmon. The third act resolution is the girls' escape from the mob.

**FACT**

A dramatic event should lead the audience to believe there is to be a climax. If the audience is not given a dramatic event scene in addition to the climax, they will leave the cinema dissatisfied. It is important not to promise what you can't deliver.

## Avoid the Machine God

As you go about creating a resolution, you don't want to fall foul of something called *deus ex machina*. That is a Latin phrase that means "god from the machine." Deus ex machina is a literary device first used

THE EVERYTHING SCREENWRITING BOOK

in Greek dramas, where the gods would come down from Mount Olympus to change the course of the action—for instance, to help resolve a difficult situation. Back then, the actors were actually lowered onto the stage by a mechanical device, hence the term "god from the machine."

While this turn of events made sense on a Greek stage, it won't make sense in today's movies. Here is an example of deus ex machina in our film about the husband's love affair: The husband doesn't leave the wife because he reads a doctor's report that he, quite by accident, discovers on top of the washing machine, which confirms that his wife is pregnant or, even worse, is suffering from a dreaded fatal disease. This ending changes the situation and takes away the man's ability to make a decision between his wife and his lover. Obviously, if his wife is severely ill he'll have to take care of her. A better resolution would be based on more realistic events.

While the plot you are working with here is not exactly bright, shiny, and original, there's no need to sink to the level of hack Hollywood, so do watch out for a deus ex machina folly.

## Real Time and Film Time

You are in the cinema, or watching a videotape at home, and on the screen you see a woman park, get out of her car, and go into a store. Then the film cuts to show the woman taking some milk from the shelves, then it cuts again and she is unlocking her car and putting a brown paper bag on the front seat. You presume, of course, that the brown bag has the milk in it.

That whole little sequence is in film time, not real time. Had the scene been shot in real time, you would probably have been getting antsy, and thinking, "This is taking forever." Shot in real time, you would have seen the woman go into the store, take a basket and look around; maybe she looked at a lot of shelves and eventually came to the milk section. Perhaps she checked the expiration date on the milk containers before she picked one. Then she went up to the checkout counter. She paid for the milk and had to wait while the cashier took time getting her change. The woman didn't seem to mind the delay. Nothing was said, but she smiled at the cashier and the cashier smiled back.

## Shooting and Editing the Scene

Let's take it for granted that the scriptwriter of the supermarket scene was writing a caper film. The woman is the girlfriend of the thief hiding out after the robbery and they need some milk. The writer was from the old school: He liked good, sharp dialogue, he wrote silences where he wanted them, he was keen on detail, and was trying to keep to real time.

**QUESTION?**

**Ever heard of a McGuffin?**
It's a term for an object that moves a story forward—a clue, such as Cinderella's glass slipper, or something desperately wanted by a character, such as the Ark of the Covenant in *Raiders of the Lost Ark*.

Maybe he had written in some tension: the woman anxiously looking over her shoulder, maybe she wasn't so calm at the checkout. However, that style didn't go down with the studio, but they didn't instruct the writer to do a rewrite; instead, they shot the long form, knowing the editor would cut it back to where they wanted it. There was nothing the writer could do; he had sold the screenplay and had been hired to do whatever smoothing out the studio wanted.

Take a minute to estimate exactly how long it would take the woman to arrive at the store, park, get the milk, and drive off. Maybe it would be somewhere around five to fifteen minutes, depending on how busy they were in the store. Edited and on the cinema screen it would probably take up a minute or so.

## A Real-Time Film

The closest any modern film has come to emulating the sequence of real time is in *High Noon*. The film was made in 1952 and starred Gary Cooper and Grace Kelly, in her first costarring part, as his wife. It was produced by Stanley Kramer, directed by Fred Zinnemann, and written by Carl Foreman. It is considered to be a classic example of the Western genre. It was nominated for seven Oscars, including Best Screenplay, and won Best Actor, Best Editing, Best Score, and Best Song awards—the song was "High Noon" ("Do Not Forsake Me, Oh My Darlin'") sung by Tex Ritter.

## Tracking the Time Frame

The running time of *High Noon* is approximately eighty-five minutes. (If you rent the videotape, record the time you start watching it. About eighty-five minutes later, THE END will come up on the screen.) Throughout, you will notice references to time passing and cuts to large clocks on walls, the hands of them ticking on toward high noon.

The action of the film, although not absolutely in time with the progress of real time, is so close that the viewer can believe the action in the film he or she is watching is the actual time of the real story being played out on the screen. This film is one of a very few where the present tense of the screenplay becomes the present tense of the viewing experience.

**FACT**

Nobody sets out to write a bad script. The same is true of books and music. No author or musician thinks that he or she should write a lousy book or song. In other words, the whole exercise is subjective. What person A loves, person B hates. Remember that when the rejections come in; all you need is to find that person A.

## Chapter 6
# Script Format

Before you start creating your master-piece, it's a good idea to have a handle on the practical aspects of writing a screenplay. The main reason for this is that over the years a film script format has evolved. When a Hollywood reader opens a screenplay, he or she expects to see all the elements of the format in place; if they're not, the first assumption is that the writer hasn't even bothered studying the industry format.

## Screenplay on Spec

Unless you are preparing a shooting script for a film that's in the works, what you are writing is a screenplay on spec—a screenplay that hasn't been commissioned. You are submitting it unsolicited in the hope that the producers will be impressed by your writing and the idea, and will make you an offer for your screenplay. Or you may submit it to an agent, who'll meet with producers on your behalf.

**ESSENTIAL**

> In all kinds of writing and publishing the author often works without any immediate financial reward; screenwriting is no different. The term *spec script* has long been a part of the Hollywood vernacular. It describes precisely what you will be doing: working on speculation.

What you have to be sure about is that you have not submitted a shooting script. Many writers go to the extent of writing in all sorts of instructions that shouldn't be there. It would be very useful to remember that the writer's job is to tell the story; it is the director who is responsible for the look and manner of the way it's told.

You will find books on bookstore shelves subtitled *The Shooting Script*. Actually, that's generally incorrect because it's not a shooting script at all. The average reader wouldn't be able to make head nor tail of a shooting script with all its scene numbers, directions, and odd pagination, with scenes in no apparent order. Your spec script is another thing and should be an easy read for any reader, in the business or not. Never be put off by simplicity; in fact, aim for it every time.

## Importance of Presentation

In an ideal world it would be marvelous if you sent in your wonderful screenplay, beautifully hand-scribed on yellow legal paper, and the reader flipped and asked you to get down to the studio ASAP to sign a contract. It's not going to happen that way. There are industry standards, and it would be a good idea if you learned to adhere to them, particularly as far as your script layout and its appearance are concerned.

If you decide to do otherwise, you shouldn't blame anyone other than yourself when your script comes back in a hurry with a note that says, in effect, thanks a lot, but no thanks. Keep in mind that these standards have been in place for a long time, and that's the way the industry works.

## Write for the Professional Reader

It may be difficult to understand, particularly if you get rejected, that what on the surface may seem to be very picky is not that way. Try to put yourself in the place of the professional reader. Imagine that you are sitting at a reader's desk in Hollywood looking at some of the junk that comes in the mail. Try to put yourself in his or her mental position. Even without any experience at all at reading submissions, you would probably reject more than half of what comes across your desk.

A professional reader very quickly gets the feel of whether or not what he or she is looking at is going to be worth the effort. This is based on the sum of the little things—even, believe it or not, simple spelling mistakes and gross grammatical errors.

The mindset of appearance is related to professionalism and image. If you happen to be substandard in that area, the reader will know you are a neophyte, and that will go against you and your work. Because this has nothing at all, at this stage, to do with the way your script has been written, it might seem unfair—but is it? Who would you rather deal with, a professional or a beginner?

**ALERT!**

Get a copy of *Topkapi,* which is a fun caper movie directed by Jules Dassin and starring his wife, Melina Mercouri. It also features Maximilian Schell and Peter Ustinov. Pay particular attention to the typical caper movie structure.

Your screenplay package is your ambassador, so it makes very good sense to be confident of its appearance, that it looks professional. It's hardly likely, for instance, that you would turn up for a job appointment in a grubby shirt and shoes in need of a shine.

Just be sure your submission looks the way it should. At the very least, you'll be sure that someone gives it a quick read. Getting your material read means you've reached first base. In any event, learning how to get the appearance of a script acceptable is the easy part; it's writing it that's tough.

# The Basic Format

The script must be written in Courier 12-point or Courier New 12-point. This is equivalent to a typewriter font of 12-point pica. (Not everyone uses a computer.) Whatever you do, keep away from what you may think are clever, fancy ploys designed to get the reader's attention, like funny colors, illustrations, odd-looking fonts, and the like. This can't be said enough times: Keep it clear and simple.

The reason for using the typewriter font is that the "one page equals one minute of screen time" rule was originally calculated on the typewriter font. That's why you want to use this font in all your scripts.

## Margins and Binding

Scripts should always be three-hole punched and held together with round-headed brass fasteners, often called *brads* (Acco is a popular brand). Just be sure that the fasteners you use are strong; you don't want your lovely script falling apart in someone's office. For some reason, it's fashionable to leave the center hole empty. The binding is the reason for the measurement of the left-hand margin—1.5 inches. The right margin should be set at 1 inch and left unjustified (ragged).

**ESSENTIAL**

Don't bother inserting ROLL CREDITS and END CREDITS into your spec script. At the time you submit your spec script, you generally don't have a clue about who else is going to be involved in the picture, and if the picture goes into production, you won't have any say in the matter anyway.

Page numbers should appear flush upper right, ½ inch from the top of the page with a double space immediately after. It's a common practice not to number page 1 (this is the same as in a manuscript of a novel).

## The Title Page

What follows is an example of a title page for a spec script. Note that this sample title page includes a note that the script is registered with the WGAw (Writers Guild of America, West). Registering your script with either the guild or the United States Copyright Office is covered in Chapter 2. On the line below that one you should type a copyright line.

The cover of your script should be 60-pound card stock, preferably in black. Put nothing on it at all. When the agents or producers or studios receive it, they will write the name of the screenplay along the spine in marker pen; don't do it yourself. Always use 8.5" × 11" white paper for the script pages.

Also on the title page in the lower right-hand corner, about 3 inches up from the bottom, are your address, phone, fax, and e-mail details. If you happen to have an agent, you would write in her or his name and address and leave your personal stuff out. All the type is in Courier New.

## Inside the Script

You'll also need to use correct notation inside the pages of your spec script. There are some scripts that may look slightly different; don't worry, the following specimen is perfectly acceptable. To see more samples, you can actually order a copy of a script for any produced film (see Appendix B for more information). Your favorite film may even be among them.

Running down from top to bottom, here is a legend to guide you: The margins should be 1.5 inches left, 1 inch right, and 1 inch top and bottom. If you get stuck with a dialogue page break (where a line of dialogue is broken up between two pages), try to adjust the top and bottom margins to fit the dialogue line into one page. The text should be single-spaced.

HERE THE TITLE OF YOUR SCREENPLAY

by

Author's Name

Registered WGAw No.xxxxx          street address

                                  city, state, zip

                                  phone number

Author's Name, YEAR              e-mail address

INT. A CLASSROOM    NIGHT


ADULT STUDENTS finding seats. The TEACHER, KATE COOPER, watches them as they settle down. She fusses with papers on her desk. She looks up.


                    COOPER
          Good evening, all. How did you get on with the
          exercise?


SIGHS and MOANS from student body.


                    NATASHA
          It was a life-warming experience.


                    COOPER
               (rolls her eyes)
          Maybe you could read it to us, Natasha.


NATASHA is a New Age woman and dresses like one.

                    NATASHA

              (clears her throat)

    The structure had the courage to be itself, it

    had lived its dream following the bliss. . .


The door of the classroom opens. A man, DOUGAN,
enters in a hurry, clutching a briefcase.


                    DOUGAN

              (with English accent)

    Do excuse me, awfully sorry I'm late.


He looks at COOPER.


                    DOUGAN

    It won't happen again, I promise.


COOPER smiles at him.


                    COOPER

    Natasha's about to read.


                    DOUGAN

    What fun.

# The Slugline

Each scene should begin with a slugline, which provides three points of information:

1. Location type: INT (interior) or EXT (exterior)
2. Location description: Any note that describes where the scene is taking place. In our sample, the location is the classroom.
3. Time of day: DAY or NIGHT (it is less common to be more specific and use DAWN, MORNING, EVENING, or DUSK).

**FACT**

Most of the time, writers are inspired by real people in their creation of characters. You may want to draw inspiration from famous actors or actresses as templates for your characters. However, do not include a cast list with your screenplay. Casting the picture is not in your domain.

The slugline is always typed in CAPS and there is a single hard return between the slugline and the next line. Here are a few other sample sluglines:

```
INT. OFFICE    DAY


EXT. PARKING LOT    DAY


INT. CHARLIE'S BEDROOM    NIGHT
```

## The Description Line

The description line, sometimes called the business line, is the text that appears flush left under the slug line and provides background and action information as to what will take place on the screen. This text should be concise and refer to what the audience would see. Here are two examples from the classroom scene you've just read:

```
ADULT STUDENTS finding seats. The
TEACHER, KATE COOPER, watches them as they
settle down. She fusses with papers on her
desk. She looks up.

NATASHA is a New Age woman and dresses
like one.
```

## Writing Dialogue

There are three parts to writing the dialogue: the character cue, parenthetical, and the dialogue line. The character cue signals the name of the character speaking and is always set in CAPS. The parenthetical is optional and signals how the character said what he said—quietly; while chewing on a piece of gum; yawning. The parenthetical may appear between the character cue and the dialogue line, or it may break up two lines of dialogue.

In the following example, the character cue is DOUGAN, the parenthetical is (with English accent), and the dialogue line is "Do excuse me. . . " A description line may also be part of the dialogue block, as in this example.

```
                    DOUGAN

              (with English accent)
         Do excuse me, awfully sorry I'm late.



       He looks at COOPER.
```

Note that unless you're using screenwriting software, you'll need to rely on tabs to indent each element. Set the character cue four tabs from the left margin, the parenthetical at three tabs, and the dialogue line at two tabs.

**ALERT!**

If you're writing a scene and you want a character to move out of shot, insert (O.S.) after the character cue when you're writing dialogue for the person off-screen. In most cases, however, you don't really need to worry about the camera work.

## Scene Transitions and Page Breaks

While some screenwriting software automatically inserts scene transitions like DISSOLVE TO, CUT TO, and FADE TO BLACK, the modern-day take by the professionals is to *never* use them in a spec script. They will signal that you are a novice, something you don't want to advertise. The same goes for (CONTINUED) or (CON'T), which some old software will enter automatically at the foot of a page.

If the software you have does that, either disable the function or change the software. If you are buying screenwriting software, be aware that the latest spec script software should not have that function.

**What happens if the industry formatting rules change?**
It's rare, but changes do take place, if for no other reason than that they suit the "in" crowd. Don't worry, but try to stay updated through networking or reading industry publications and recently written screenplays.

## Practice by Reading

All these directions will get less confusing if you pick up a script and read through it. After a while, you'll get used to the formatting and it'll come easier to you as you begin to write on your own. Pick a film you particularly want to study and see if you can get hold of a copy of its screenplay. Once you read the screenplay, rent the movie, and see how the writing comes alive on the screen.

It doesn't always help to stick with the best films. Sometimes it's also educational to see films that failed, because you can learn from the failures how to avoid making the same mistakes.

## More of the Don'ts

Somehow it seems that in the Hollywood game there are more things one *shouldn't* do than one should do. This certainly seems to be the case with the creation of a screenplay. Here are a few more of the things you should stay away from:

- Never write "We see him open the door." "We sees" are out.
- Avoid references to the camera, such as "The camera shows the aerial view of the barn."
- Never repeat the information in the slugline.
- Avoid first-person action (using "I" or "we").
- Never write action in the past tense.

# Using Your Computer

Today it is part and parcel of putting words to paper to be at least marginally computer literate. Whatever we may think about the computer, it is an established part of all businesses, including the film business.

If you are well educated in the computer world, you could design a template layout for your word-processing program that uses key codes like ALT–S to shift formats from slugline to character cue and so forth. Otherwise, your options are to do formatting manually, relying on cutting and pasting, or to familiarize yourself with a screenwriting program.

## Software Programs

A software program designed for screenwriting will make your job much easier. If you are seriously planning to write, it may be well worth the expense. (Appendix B provides two software options, and there are others on the market.) It'll help you keep track of all the material, give you various searching options, minimize the busywork of retyping the character cues and other repeating tags, and save all your revisions, so that you can choose to "undo" the changes at any time.

**ALERT!**

Your script has to be easy to read. A cluttered, messy script is going to get dumped in a hurry. Remember, a professional reader is not going to submit anything he or she knows the boss isn't going to like. The professional's report is going to consist of a couple of sharp pages.

As with all software programs, the promotional material that comes with screenwriting software programs will tell you how easy life is going to be once you have loaded their goodies. But be forewarned: You will have to do more than breathe on the screen for your screenplay software to start producing. There is going to be a learning curve. How long that will take depends on you, of course.

Luckily, many software companies now offer trial versions that you can download and use for a short while. This way, you can familiarize yourself with the program and what it will allow you to do—as well as how difficult it will be to use—before you make the commitment to purchase it.

Irrespective of which kind of technique you adopt, never let it out of your mind that what is going to impress people in the long run is the content of what you write. Follow all the advice about presentation because it's essential, but once you are over that hurdle it's what's in the package that counts.

# Chapter 7
# Writing Scenes

You have done all your research and decided on the story/concept that might claim to hold the attention of a potential agent or perhaps a Hollywood reader, and you understand how script layout works. Now it's time to begin the actual process of writing. In order to make your task less daunting, you can tackle the process one scene at a time.

## Some Advice Before You Begin

It cannot be stressed enough that the approach to your first serious spec screenplay has to be simple, yet dynamic. It is essential that you concentrate on "seeing" the images that the words you write make. Avoid being fast and loose with words, except in dialogue—provided it is appropriate to the character. Because the word usage in scripts tends to be limited, the ones that are used have to be specific. A word communicates a message; be sure that you have control over what the message is meant to be.

**QUESTION?**

**Why is it that scriptwriters and directors all seem to feud?**
The simplest answer is to say that not all of them do, but when they do, it usually has to do with their control over the movie. The power of the director has evolved over the years and the cost of film production has put the onus of success on the director, and sometimes the screenwriters feel left out of the project.

## A Scene Outline

Let's presume that you have more than just an idea of how your script is going to proceed. You have mapped out the three acts, keeping in mind that whatever you set up in the first act is going to affect how the third act plays out.

To help you get started, it may help to create a scene outline. Some writers get a set of index cards and label each card as a specific scene. Then they can lay the cards out in the order in which the scenes will appear in the movie. This is useful because when you make revisions, you can simply move the order of the cards around. This way, you can visualize the progression of the movie and see what has already happened and what is yet to take place.

Each basic scene should perform the following:

• Move the story forward.
• Move the main character closer to or further away from his or her goal.

- Add to viewers' understanding of the character.
- Have a beginning, a middle, and an end.
- Be a logical and necessary part of the story.
- Show how the characters involved feel.
- Be compelling—contain either conflict or the foreshadowing of it, or show an unexpected alliance between opponents.
- Keep viewers eager to learn what happens next.

Once you've got a basic outline of your scenes, you'll have to pick the first one to start working on. It doesn't necessarily have to be the first scene, which is arguably the most important scene of the screenplay. In fact, you can start out small, writing small connecting scenes that would appear later in the film.

## The First Scene

One of your most important objectives is now going to be the drafting of the first ten pages—the deadly ten. Roughly, this is what happens when a reader picks up your spec script. First of all, the reader gauges the overall appearance of the script, maybe flipping over a few pages to establish that the writer knows how to format a spec script. If all that looks as if the writer knows what he or she is up to, then it's directly to the first page, which should begin with FADE IN.

**ALERT!** Avoid long stretches of monologue and lengthy expositions. The best way to introduce background material is through dialogue or to show it on-screen. And in many cases indirect hints work better than obviously stated facts.

Let's say your script has passed stage one. Now the reader wants to find out what the story is about. The reader's eyes scan the opening scene. Remember, you have only ten minutes—ten pages—to grab and hold the reader; otherwise, your script is moved to the rejection pile.

What are you going to include in your first ten pages? How are you planning to introduce your characters? How soon are you going to introduce the first master scene? (A master scene is a complete set of actions that take place in one location.)

## The Master Scene

The most straightforward, simple, and easy-to-understand method of constructing a script is by building on master scenes. The following is the first master scene of the film *Loophole*, which has previously been used to provide examples.

What can the reader deduce from reading this page? First, that the picture must be a caper flick. Second, the character named Mike Daniels must be in the lead; supporting actors would play the other two men in the scene. The scene is about a page long, which means it would run for about a minute.

If in doubt, cut it out. Learn to trust your intuition; if you get a gut feeling that something isn't working for some reason, don't fret endlessly over it—get rid of it and see whether what you've written plays better with the cut. Invariably, the piece will be improved.

Note that the scene was mostly action, with little dialogue—in fact, only one of the three men spoke, so the conversation was one-sided. Note, too, that there was no sight of the safe being robbed and money being taken. All that was left to the audience's imagination.

Try to remember that you will involve the audience if you allow them to contribute to the story. You do that by not writing in every detail under the sun.

```
INT.  WAREHOUSE    LONDON    NIGHT
```

MIKE DANIELS is crouched over a large SAFE. A thin beam of light cuts through the blackness to show the keyhole of the safe.

A THIN MAN holds a FLASHLIGHT. A short FAT MAN stands by a window that is covered by black felt. A BLACK CAT is crouching low over the floor; its tail lashes in anger.

Daniels feeds a DETONATOR into the keyhole and tapes it.

                    DANIELS
          That should do it. You can cover up now.

He watches the THIN MAN covering the door of the safe.

                    DANIELS
          Funny stuff, nitro. You got to watch it.
          Like fat men, it sweats with old age.

The THIN MAN steps away from the safe. Daniels goes to it and trails detonator wire across the floor into an office.

                        DANIELS

     Right, then.


     The three men crouch behind a desk in the office.

     There is a muffled ROAR. A filing-cabinet drawer

     slides open. The cat SCREECHES, jumps in the air,

     and runs out of sight.


     The three men smile at each other.

## Breaking Down the Scene

Just as the screenplay as a whole has a beginning, middle, and end, so too should each individual scene. Look at the sample scene again. It opens on a safe in a dark warehouse, obviously at night. A beam of light shows a man crouching over the safe. That's the beginning. (A robbery is in progress.)

Then we see two other men who have to be helping the first man. The angry cat adds to the atmosphere. Now we get the business with the detonator. The dialogue lets the audience know that nitroglycerin is involved. (Most adults in the audience would know what nitro means and is used for.) The detonator wire is laid into place and the three men take shelter behind the desk. That's the middle.

Guess what? The end is the explosion and the smiles from the crooks that show the safe has blown. There are two bits of business: The filing-cabinet drawer opening of its own volition and the cat screeching and running off—hence, the beginning, middle, and end of the scene. We now would move on to the next scene.

Ask yourself if this scene fulfills the needs of a good scene. Does it move the story forward, provide the information the audience needs to understand the story, and engage their interest? If it does all of that, you are well on your way. You have created a building block of your story.

# A Breakdown of Shots

Even a scene as short as our first master scene would have to be broken down into camera shots. It is here that the style and artistry of the director can come into play. You might start off doing this yourself, to practice visualizing the scene in a film. Try figuring out how the director may want to approach showing Daniels bending over the safe and following the scene on through to the explosion.

**QUESTION?**

**What if you want to add a voice-over to a particular scene?** If you have a character or narrator making commentary from outside of the scene—for instance, your character may be telling a story or looking back at an episode in his or her life—you should treat the voice-over as dialogue, but insert (V.O.) following the character cue.

Would the establishing shot be wide to show Daniels, the safe, and the other two actors, or would it be tighter, showing only Daniels, then pulling back to open up the scene? The storyboarding would show that. The director may well show his storyboards to the cast during rehearsal.

## Storyboarding

Many directors storyboard their scripts, even if they can hardly draw. Hitchcock was, perhaps, the most famous director who storyboarded his scripts. In fact, he went so far as to say that the actual shooting was boring because he had already shot the film in his head.

What is storyboarding? It's the process of producing sketches of the shots of your script. Notice that storyboarding breaks down the film into shots, not scenes. Had our hypothetical director done this to the opening scene at the safe, he or she would have played with the camera angles.

One reason why directors do not want to see scripts that detail camera setups and angles is because they get in their way. However, if you are in any doubt about how you want your scene to play, even though you don't write it in the script, it might be worthwhile to storyboard the scene for your own benefit. You could even use small puppets or dolls (borrow your kids' Barbie dolls, if you have to) and set them up to see how you think they could be placed and moved in the scene.

The actors would only move around if you write the scene in such a way that it is simply logical for a certain character to move, stand up, sit down, and so on. Just see that the action in the scene justifies the movement. Then it's doubtful the director would call you on it. Of course, what you can't storyboard are the inner emotions of your characters, but you can write their reactions.

**Try to get a copy of *Rear Window,* directed by Alfred Hitchcock. Pay attention to how one scene flows into the next. Remember, Hitchcock was famous for storyboarding his films.**

Try to remember when you write that you are the one most intimate with what you mean. Double-check yourself to make sure that what you mean is communicated by the words you write, so that other people will get the same drift. As the book says: Write confusingly clearly.

## Making Sure the Scenes Flow

The scene that follows next takes place in the working-class home of Mike Daniels, where the money from the robbery is being shared out. Daniels's wife has sandwiches and drinks all ready for the guys. The audience will learn that they have two children. This is how the character development begins. Note that the best way of presenting character development information is by showing.

Because of the way Daniels and his wife treat each other and because the scene is typical of any marital situation when the wife welcomes her husband and his coworkers home, this sets the tone for how the audience will relate to the characters—as real people they could relate to, not the bad-guy thugs. The image of Daniels will be that he is not just some slick thief, but a married man with a home and responsibilities.

## Laying the Development Groundwork

Daniels proposes the next robbery; in fact, we all learn that the one just carried out was staged to finance an upcoming big one. The others are amazed because what Daniels is proposing is a robbery everyone said could never be pulled off. Here, not all members of the group are convinced that Daniels is right and some have to be convinced. Human nature being what it is, though, the audience will want Daniels to succeed; the fascination will be if and how he does.

Daniels discloses that he already has the rest of the crew lined up. All he is missing is a technical expert; the robbery is to be carried out by going through the London sewer system.

So far we probably have no more than three to four minutes on the screen. This is time enough for the audience to have started sizing up the people/actors they have met so far. Do they like them, even though they are crooks?

While it's not essential for the audience to like all the characters, the scriptwriter should try to create characters that elicit an appropriate reaction—whether it is sympathy or dislike. The writer might turn to real life and the people he or she knows to use as templates for created characters.

## Chronological Progression

It should come as no big surprise that the next scene introduces the technical expert, Stephen Booker, who happens to be a laid-off architect driving a cab while he fruitlessly tries to get another job. Daniels has been using the cab to get to know this man, whose marriage is faltering because of the lack of income.

# Chapter 8

# The Protagonist

The term *protagonist* comes from the Greek words *protos* (first) and *agonistes* (actor or combatant). The protagonist is the principal player, the lead, and the star of the show. In film, the protagonist must be a dynamic character who drives the action and must resolve the conflict, which propels the plot.

## The Main Attraction

You might say that the lead player in a script is the first character layer of the plot or story line, because the story line must in some way revolve around this person. Ideally, a strong star and a strong plot should be mutually involved. A weak character linked to a weak plot will almost certainly produce a disaster; neither alone will save the day. Ask yourself how many times you have seen a film with a blockbuster star that is a total flop.

Analyzing a flop can be a valuable exercise because it can provide clues on what not to do. The first question you might ask is how is it that with all this talent the film is no good? It must be more than the star having a bad day. As Hamlet said, "The play's the thing," and it certainly is the rock on which all else rests. The scriptwriter's first job, therefore, is the creation of this solid base from which a star can flourish.

**FACT**

Because making a great film depends in large part on the actors, particularly the star, the scriptwriter has the prime responsibility—to provide the elements of expression for the actors. Only if the scriptwriter does his or her job properly will the actors be able to shine.

The protagonist is a character who has to generate emotional energy in the audience. The emotion can be positive or negative, as long as it's a strong reaction. It can range all the way from the villain you love to hate to the hero you would die for. The worst sin a scriptwriter can commit is to create a protagonist who is blah, who registers a zero on the emotion scale.

## Creating the Lead Character

First, of course, you start with the subject of the story you have created. It will be the story that generally dictates the type of protagonist you will create. Nevertheless, whatever the genre of your concept and whatever the plot, the gamut of personality is still wide open. This is particularly so if you wish to make a protagonist who is not a stereotypical figure, but is created against the grain.

**ALERT!**

Another piece of movie business vernacular you should learn is "character arc," the imaginary curved line that represents the development of a character's passage through the screenplay. The character arc is supposed to shape and change the character as he or she progresses through the plot.

Many films that have a professional person as the protagonist—a priest, a cop, a newspaper writer, and such—tend to emphasize the totally positive and clichéd aspects of the character instead of producing a rounded-out profile. Probably the most questionable example of this was a film called *Going My Way*, which beat out *Double Indemnity* in the 1944 Oscar awards. In *Going My Way*, the lead is a crooning, golf-playing New York priest, Bing Crosby, who not only saves the souls of his rough-and-tumble parish but also wins over the antagonist, who holds the mortgage on the church. Barry Fitzgerald doesn't help by playing a fellow priest in his established crotchety leprechaun way.

## A More Realistic Approach

A more realistic religious example might be the Catholic priest character in Alfred Hitchcock's *I Confess* (1953), with Montgomery Clift. Set in Quebec, Canada, the film was based on a play by Paul Anthelme, *Nos deux consciences*. Although not one of Hitchcock's best, it does serve as a good example of how a characterization of a standard and potentially clichéd figure doesn't come off that way. This priest has doubts; he is not perfect and realizes it. That he has flaws makes his character more believable.

The conflict in the film becomes apparent early on. A German refugee and his wife work in a Catholic church. The husband murders a lawyer. He goes to confession in his own church and is heard by the Catholic priest. Subsequently, the priest is arrested for the murder; there is a possible motive. The priest, therefore, has to choose between the sanctity of the confessional and saving himself.

The tension is generated between the murderer and the priest, each of whom, obviously, knows the truth. A secondary plot line of a woman, Anne Baxter, who loves the priest, adds to the mix. The ending is contrived from the point of view that the priest doesn't have to get down to the wire of breaking his vows, because the real murderer is discovered—actually, he gets shot inside the church by the police. As he dies, he cries out: "Forgive me, father."

## The Hard-Boiled Protagonist

Here is another type of protagonist—this one is clearly a stereotype. This character is the hard-boiled investigator, a seasoned private eye. This character is a personality born from the early days of the pulp magazines that evolved in the same way and time that the film noir genre developed, both in books and the movies. The picture of a man in a trench coat became synonymous with the private eye. Alan Ladd, who went on to star in *Shane*, epitomized the genre in *This Gun for Hire*.

Many private-eye characters were former cops who have good connections with the law, both in the police force and the lawyer business. They were not held in high esteem by these professions; rather, they were tolerated. They were single men, generally, and their backgrounds were typically shrouded in mystery, and thus were romantic. They were smart, but often their intelligence was concealed behind a brusque, quick-talking, smart-ass façade.

They were licensed to carry arms and if the situation really called for it, they had no qualms about using them. They were not necessarily tough, but they knew how to take punishment and come back, sometimes for more. They treated women with respect but with caution; the long-term commitment was not part of their modus operandi. They lived alone, smoked cigarettes or a pipe, and they drank, usually inexpensive Scotch; they took their coffee black. As you can see, you can't get more stereotypical than the private-eye character.

Movie stars that made their names as hard-boiled characters included Humphrey Bogart, Alan Ladd, Robert Mitchum, Edward G. Robinson,

James Cagney, Sterling Hayden, and Robert Ryan. Actresses, too, may be included in the hard-boiled category. In particular, Ida Lupino, Barbara Stanwyck, Joan Crawford, and Mercedes McCambridge distinguished themselves in hard-boiled character roles.

It might be said that directing and screenwriting are the two most important elements in the production of a successful film, and some are good at both. For instance, Billy Wilder received eight Oscar nominations for directing and twelve for screenwriting.

## The Villain They Love to Hate

In romantic comedy stories, it might be surprising to some that the audience will usually root for the cad over the clean-cut hero. To a few people, this doesn't seem logical, but the screenplay is usually on the side of the underdog, who gets the girl in the end.

### The Antihero

The antihero isn't exactly a villain. He is a hero who lacks positive qualities that you normally associate with the protagonist. Some hard-boiled protagonists are in fact antiheroes. They are far too cynical to come off as brave, honest, and unselfish, though by the end of the film they'll win the affections of the audience—and perhaps of the female lead as well. Ironically, it's their antihero qualities that endear them to the viewers.

The antihero philosophy is summed up nicely in a line spoken by one of the movies' top antiheros, Rick (played by Humphrey Bogart), in *Casablanca*. It's delivered in reply to Inspector Renault's warning about Ungarte, a character played by Peter Lorre, who is to be arrested in Rick's place for the murder of two German couriers who were carrying the letters of transit. As Rick put it, "I stick my neck out for nobody."

# The Protagonist Drives Action

It is the accepted theory that action follows the protagonist. The protagonist generates the conflict. Everything to do with its development and resolution revolves around the protagonist, too. In short, the protagonist is the man or woman at the center of attention. It shouldn't take too much analysis to figure out that the protagonist has to be the sort of character who can hold everyone's attention.

There are a number of ways a character gets to the audience. This depends, in part, on the actor who plays the main lead. As most evolving scriptwriters will be writing spec scripts, there is little chance of knowing in advance who will be cast to play their hero or heroine. Even sadder is the fact that the bigger the star, the more likely rewrites will be ordered up, and they probably won't be done by the screenwriter. As you write your characters, remember that the better your script, the less rewriting will have to be done to fit the actors who are going to play the character parts.

A lead character can't be separated from the action, nor the other way around. There are a couple of ways the character becomes involved in action: Either he or she instigates it or is the recipient of it. In whatever way this comes about, it will usually involve other people—supporting characters.

**QUESTION?**

**Isn't any movement, like a woman walking across a room, considered to be an action?**
It's an action, but it's not action. Action in a script is designed to accomplish something more substantial in the way of forward movement of the story line. Every scene you create should only have material in it that helps move the story forward. Otherwise, out it goes.

## Writing Action

For the sake of illustration, let's not deal with pure action films. The reason for this is that they are mostly the armed-conflict type of action without too much in the way of subtlety. What actually constitutes action? One answer might be that it is the movement in the screenplay from an initial entanglement, progressing through rising action to a climax that results in falling action that leads to the resolution. (As you should already know, that is another way of expressing that the structure of the screenplay is in three acts.)

Like conflict, almost anything can produce action. Take a simple situation: A registered letter from a debtor threatening legal action arrives at the protagonist's home. The character sits down to read the letter. The room is well and tastefully furnished. The man is good-looking and dressed in chinos, topsiders, and an open-necked checked shirt.

The man looks up to the window because he can hear his children playing outside; he registers worry and concern. The door to the room opens and his wife comes in. She is wearing white tennis gear. She's an attractive woman.

The wife is curious to know what's in the letter. The husband passes it to her. She reads it and reacts: "What the hell are you gonna do about this one?" The husband doesn't answer; he puts his head in his hands. Thus, a letter starts a chain of events. Even if this were the first scene in the picture, the audience is already gathering valuable information.

**ESSENTIAL**

> The finest plot will not hold the interest of an audience unless they care about the characters in it. They must want to know and care what is going to happen to the people up there on the screen. To keep an audience entranced for a hundred minutes, they must be engaged by what they're watching.

They obviously know the family is in financial trouble and that the husband is not at work. Without consciously knowing it, they have also absorbed the social strata of the couple: they live in a very nice home, they have some children who are playing in a garden, they are wearing typical upwardly mobile clothes, and they look good in them. Having taken that in, the audience has added to it their own opinions, which are subject to their experiences as well as their prejudices—the audience brings everything they are to the viewing. It is important that the scriptwriter realizes what is going on in the viewers' minds.

## Another Version

Using exactly the same scene plot, let's look at how an audience might react if only a few of the details were changed. A man is sitting in a room reading a letter. The room is cluttered with junk; in one corner there are stacks of unread newspapers. The man is wearing old jeans and a workingman's shirt; he needs a shave. The man looks up to the window and grimaces at the loud noise some children are making; he takes out a cigarette and lights it.

The door opens and a woman comes in. She is wearing an old dress with an apron tied around her waist. Her hair is long and unkempt. She looks at the letter. "You got another of them damn demand things?" The man doesn't look up. He drags on his cigarette and lets ash from it fall on the floor. He tears the letter in two. "I just put it in the pending file."

Rent a copy of *The Odd Couple* (1968), written by Neil Simon, starring Jack Lemmon and Walter Matthau. Apart from being an absolute hoot, it's a fine example of how the dialogue suits each character and contributes to their diametrically opposed characterizations.

The odds are that if the same actors were handed those two sets of script pages, they would get more of a kick out of playing the rough, lower-class couple than the upwardly mobile twosome. This doesn't mean that one setup is better than the other, only that characters who seem to have more "character" are more interesting both to play and to watch. Either way, filmmakers, actors, and audiences want to feel emotionally involved with the people the scriptwriter has invented.

# Speaking of the Stars

Compared with a novelist, the playwright and the scriptwriter have it easy. Whereas the novelist has to go it alone and write in all the nuances of character and utterance throughout the book, the playwright and scriptwriter rely on actors to interpret their roles.

The industry annually lists the top box-office movie stars, which can be interpreted to read: the most bankable. Below is one list; the names will change from year to year, according to subsequent box-office success or decline. The average payment to anyone on the list hovers around the $10 to $20 million mark per picture. It doesn't take too much to understand the tremendous importance and value that a good screenplay has to these players.

- Tom Cruise
- Tom Hanks
- Julia Roberts
- Mel Gibson
- Jim Carrey
- George Clooney
- Russell Crowe
- Harrison Ford
- Bruce Willis
- Brad Pitt

**FACT**

While nobody seems to be able to track down the exact source, it is a fact that an actor originally named Bernie Schwartz took a scriptwriter's prose and delivered this interpretation: "Yonder lies duh castle of my Fadah, duh King." The actor would later make his name as Tony Curtis.

These listings that come out of Hollywood shouldn't depress the average scriptwriter; there are hundreds of pictures produced every year, and certainly not all of them are in Hollywood, so there are plenty of chances for us all. At the same time, while it may on the surface seem to be a plus having a star playing a part you wrote, who is to say the part will be read the way you want it to be read? That's a chance every scriptwriter has to face. It's all part of the business.

## Star Power

Frequently, it is the star, the potential protagonist, who will be the most influential in getting a script off the ground and into production. Because this is an established method of raising the money for the budget, the description "bankable" came about. "So and so is a bankable star," it will be said, meaning, of course, that the star has clout in the business. Clout in Hollywood is earned and measured by box-office success, the sole criteria.

Stars and their advisors can spend endless weeks scanning submitted scripts in an effort to find a suitable one. This isn't just looking at scripts that were deliberately written with a particular star in mind, but for projects that might be right for a change the star wishes to make in his or her career path. Perhaps it is felt the dreaded typecast label is being bandied about too often.

However, in spite of that and for various other reasons, a story/script might be created solely for a special actor or actress. This can be seen today with the proliferation of sequels, series, or knock-offs, most of which tend to dilute the original attraction and at best dribble off into the video wasteland. What is often not realized by the public is that actors and actresses want to work and often they cut corners to do so; also, the money's not that bad. Whatever the reasons, it shouldn't be forgotten that there are always lead players who wish to stretch their talents and try something new.

## The Star As a Template

Although it is rare that the scriptwriter has the opportunity to actually write for a movie star, there is no harm in basing your protagonist on a specific actor—it will help you envision your character and the way he or she behaves and speaks. Many writers use existing stars as the template for the protagonist in a spec script. The hope is, of course, that the script is picked up by an agent who sees how well-suited the great script is to this big star, and the phones start humming.

Looked at from a creative point of view, there is a downside to the idea. You may be so taken up with a certain star that your script turns out to be a valentine to them. That is probably not going to work. If you objectively pick a star as a template, that might work; either way, you should act in exactly the same manner as you would when creating any protagonist.

Your first step on the research path is to establish whom you think might welcome a good script that was tailored for them; not all stars would. Check on stars who keep doing the same kind of picture, and check on those whose talents obviously outstrip the material they've been doing. That list might be a long one. Eventually, you will have narrowed your list down to a manageable size: if you're lucky, a list of one.

The best way to approach the project is not to get too involved in the idea that you are writing a script for a fabulous star. Just write the script the best way you can, as if you had penciled out a protagonist based on an amalgam of a couple of your friends. Don't sit at your keyboard trying to figure how Tom or Julia or whomever would handle a scene. Work out how your protagonist would do it.

**FACT**

"The bigger problem is that there are so few leading men now. There's no Gable, no more Spencer Tracy, Gary Cooper . . . there used to be a list of leading men. Now there are only three or four. Who are you going to write for, unless it's Tom Cruise?"
—Cameron Crowe, from *Conversations with Wilder.*

## Chapter 9

# Supporting Characters

Once you've developed your protagonist, it's time to look at the other characters in your story. As you write characters, it's important to visualize them in your mind. You should know their motivations, their backgrounds, and their goals, even if they will never be stated or even hinted at in the story. The way you develop supporting or secondary characters is through their participation in the plot by way of action and dialogue.

## The Role of Supporting Characters

The depth and strength of the supporting character is relative to his or her place in the plot. Many times a character acts as the foil for the protagonist, bouncing off or interacting with him or her. These characters stand out, but don't detract from the protagonist's domination of the story and the screen. Famous comedy foils tend to act as the "feed" to their "straight" partner. Examples are: Abbott and Costello, Martin and Lewis, Laurel and Hardy.

**FACT**

Three entirely different actors can play the same part and there will be three entirely different results. If a writer is lucky, he or she will get an actor who goes after the life of the character.

Another manifestation of the supporting character is as the confidant (or confidante). The confidant can be a close friend of the protagonist and privy to his or her private thoughts and problems. For the scriptwriter, this can be a useful device in that the protagonist can tell inner thoughts to the confidant without boring the audience with personal monologues. As you can see, having secondary characters can often help you solve the problem of sharing crucial information about what's going on without resorting to exposition or obviousness.

## Naming Your Characters

The first step in creating dialogue for a character who stands a chance of actually remaining in the script is the character's name. While a rose by any other name may smell as sweet, if it could speak it wouldn't sound the same. Try dreaming up some off-the-wall names, then imagine what kind of dialogue you would write for characters with these names.

The names people have in real life frequently don't seem to fit them; have you ever met someone and later thought that they don't act and talk like a Bambi or a Rod? The language coming from a Blanche DuBois would probably not sound anything like the language coming from a

Gertie Entwhistle. Remember a song called "A Boy Named Sue?"

Unless you are involved in writing an adaptation, where you are more or less obliged to use existing character names, give a lot of thought to the names you pick. Relate your choice to the kind of personality you want to project. Keep in mind that the language you eventually create for these characters should be closely allied to the kind of person they are meant to be. Most obviously, their names should signal their background. However, there are plenty of other ways to communicate information through a character's name. Nicknames work particularly well here, as do aliases. Quentin Tarantino found a creative way to use aliases in his film *The Reservoir Dogs*, where characters mask their anonymity with names like Mr. Pink, Mr. Blue, and Mr. Orange.

**QUESTION?**

**Has the movie culture changed? If so, in what way?**
Yes, it has, just as society has changed. The change was brought by computer technology and what came with it. But nothing will change the acceptance of a good story. Good stories are made by good writers, whether they use a computer or paper and pencil.

## Characters Are Shaped by Dialogue

In the theater, words spoken onstage by actors are referred to as *language*. What the screenwriter has to learn is the language spoken in films. Bad movie dialogue—and there's a lot of it—sounds as if the words were assigned, not spontaneously thought up by the character. On the other hand, good dialogue will describe a character and often pick that person out in a crowd of stereotypes.

You should give a lot of thought to the background of the characters you are going to create. Where are they from, what are their parents like, and what did they do before their appearance on the screen? Think of your own background. How has it shaped what you are today, what you want, the way you speak, and so forth? You can do the same for each character you create—just use your imagination or use people you know for inspiration.

## Avoid Cliché Hell

You now have to give some serious thought to the question of cliché and originality. In scripts the dialogue is often what the Hollywood reader would expect to hear from the characters in the situations in which the writer has placed them. That's all very well, and the reader would probably let it go by without too much of a thought, but supposing you had created some fresh, original dialogue?

**FACT**

A strong character who is well drawn will never sound the same as another character. A strong personality will rarely produce weak language. By the same token, a weak person will rarely produce strong language unless he or she has somehow been provoked. It is personality that produces individual language.

Presuming you are writing a spec script, the choice is yours. The question is: Should you take a chance? Will your take be that originality and freshness (provided it's linked to a strong story) will carry you forward, so that the reader will be entranced with your creativity? It's a good thought and one that can't be put aside, because the idea of something fresh coming about is rare, and some say sorely needed. It's not only in dialogue that you will find the cliché; characters who speak in clichés are that way, too.

## Working with and Against Assumptions

Audiences expect characters who they think they have identified to act in a certain manner. They do this in two ways. First of all, they may recognize the actor from other films. Secondly, they'll make assumptions based on the way an actor they don't know looks, acts, and speaks. They do this by matching the collection of signs the actor is sending, which to them adds up to a character profile they have stored in their brain. This is why an eyewitness is the worst kind of witness you would ever want to meet in a dark alley. That is perhaps the way stereotypes are created; for instance, all Mafia mobsters look and act like the people in *The Godfather* or the television series knock-off *The Sopranos*. This kind of stereotyping leads to a faulty social education, because few people actually know what a Mafia family is like.

Screenwriters over forty years old and without an established track record often take great pains not to give away their age. Being a mature writer in Hollywood is not a plus. The degree of wisdom that maturity generally brings doesn't rate. Fortunately, writers don't have to be too visible—until they pick up their Oscar, that is.

Other stereotypes are more deeply entrenched in our society and have been around for centuries. It's long been a common, if unconscious, belief that people with red hair are more likely to have bad tempers. Serious people who don't smile often are either perpetually angry or mean. These kinds of stereotypes have been around since the age of Shakespeare, who got into the act when he had Julius Caesar say of a chap called Cassius: "Let me have men about me that are fat, / Sleek-headed men and such as sleep a-nights. / Yond Cassius has a lean and hungry look, / He thinks too much; such men are dangerous."

It's an accepted fact that most of us form first cursory opinions about other people based on what are really a collection of marginal observations. Sometimes you can actually use this to your advantage and fool the audience. Let's say you have a male character who gives all the appearances of being a very upstanding, clean-cut, reliable sort of fellow. Don't overdo it and make him too good for words; instead, just make him a regular sort of guy, the type who would organize the local soccer league, or be active in his local church.

Then, write a scene in which this character hosts a dinner. The scene opens as the guests arrive. The audience sees the wife and maybe the children, before they scuttle out of sight. Everyone is having a great time and the impression is that this is a high-quality group of people.

At this point the audience should be sold on the characterization of the character; there should be no clues written in to change their impressions. Dinner is over, and coffee is being served. A male guest looks over at the protagonist and just slightly raises his eyebrows. The protagonist looks to another part of the room and does the same to another male guest.

**QUESTION?**

**How subtle do you have to be to fool audiences?**
Never underestimate the audience; remember, they have probably seen a lot of films. If you are too obvious, the chances are they will see through your ploy. Try to write so that they contribute to their own conclusions without you "telling" them.

At this point everything is open, and any kind of action can ensue. It's all in the hands of the scriptwriter. What's going on in this proper upper-middle-class house? Is it not quite what was first thought? Only the scriptwriter knows what'll come next.

## Stereotypical Groups

The problem with the stereotypical character or group is that they themselves adhere to the established image. So what is the option if you want to write yet another Mafia flick? Maybe a WASP Godfather isn't going to work too well. Will the audience find this character believable? Or will the switch shock them out of the illusion of the film? Sometimes the decision to stick with stereotypes should depend on how realistic you want to be, whether you want to show true character or the dramatic one Hollywood would prefer.

What compounds the group cliché situation is that the groups tend to attach themselves to the image projected by movies; each feeds off the other until nobody knows who originated what. Probably the best a scriptwriter can aim for is to inject a new slant to the established stereotype.

## Do Your Research

There is a frequent criticism written in reviews about some films that the characters—particularly minor roles and those of minorities or women—are one-dimensional. The critique is often justified, and not only because the writer is perceived as being deliberately prejudicial. More likely than not, the screenwriter was simply being lazy and didn't think. This kind of writing hardly qualifies as professional.

The basis of the problem can actually be one of sloppy research and the reliance on stereotypes. It shouldn't come as a surprise that research is required if you are going to have characters in your screenplay who are not reflections of the kind of person you are or you know. Obviously, you can't have all your characters be miniature versions of your own self, so it's important to do your research. Movies and television will help if you want to write stereotypes, but to really get at a character, your best bet is to go out and talk to people. If you are writing a police detective story, it won't hurt to visit the local police station.

Forrest Gump was the epitome of an original, and perhaps even unique, character. There was certainly no one else in the picture remotely like him. The character was based on the one in Winston Groom's book. It was an excellent example of consistency of characterization. The screenplay was by Eric Roth.

As with all personal research, you will get a lot more from it than you went for. The way to carry out successful research is to watch and listen. You can practice by writing characters who are diametrically the opposite of yourself. If you are a man in your fifties, try writing a teenage girl character. If you are a young woman, how about a character of an old man? Try changing the economic status, geographic location, and personality traits. If you stumble on a good character, you can use him or her in your screenplay.

## Learn from Supporting Actors

More than most, supporting players in movies, also known as *character actors,* easily become typecast; in fact with many that is their attraction. Hence the saying "He or she is right out of central casting." Audiences will frequently see the same actors or actresses turning up playing a similar part, although in a wide variety of pictures.

## Favorite Supporting Players

There are times when the supporting player in a film is considered to be the better actor/actress in the entire production. Some movie aficionados get to the stage of making their own list of their favorite supporting players. Here is a short one covering the eight years between 1994 and 2001—Oscar winners for best supporting actress:

**2002:**    Catherine Zeta-Jones, *Chicago*
**2001:**    Jennifer Connelly, *A Beautiful Mind*
**2000**:    Marcia Gay Harden, *Pollock*
**1999:**    Angelina Jolie, *Girl, Interrupted*
**1998:**    Dame Judi Dench, *Shakespeare in Love*
**1997:**    Kim Basinger, *L.A. Confidential*
**1996:**    Juliette Binoche, *The English Patient*
**1995:**    Mira Sorvino, *Mighty Aphrodite*
**1994:**    Dianne Wiest, *Bullets over Broadway*

And, for the same period, Oscar winners for best supporting actor:

**2002:**    Chris Cooper, *Adaptation*
**2001:**    Jim Broadbent, *Iris*
**2000:**    Benicio Del Toro, *Traffic*
**1999:**    Michael Caine, *The Cider House Rules*
**1998:**    James Coburn, *Affliction*
**1997:**    Robin Williams, *Good Will Hunting*
**1996:**    Cuba Gooding, Jr., *Jerry Maguire*
**1995:**    Kevin Spacey, *The Usual Suspects*
**1994:**    Martin Landau, *Ed Wood*

Such is memory that perhaps you might be pushed to rent one of the pictures listed. Maybe you didn't see it in the year it won the award.

## Balancing the Characters

They don't have a category in the Oscars called Best Supporting Actor for nothing. That is a specific award title, which a person like Clint Eastwood has yet to win. Once that is well established in your mind, you can start thinking about balance. The balance needs to be between the protagonist and the supporting or "character" actors.

> Take a look at *On the Waterfront* (1954), starring Marlon Brando, directed by Elia Kazan, with a script by Budd Schulberg. Terry Malloy as the protagonist has a number of supporting actors around him, all of whom are superbly and strongly played. It's a wonderful example of multiple supporting characters.

Major characters should have inner lives and a three-dimensional development. Major characters can change as the picture progresses; in fact, it's preferable that they do. Minor characters tend not to embrace those aspects, which isn't to say they are cardboard cutouts. It's just that they generally don't have the same degree of depth. In other words, they don't undergo any significant change, because they aren't involved in creating change in others or in events.

Never confuse lack of change with shallowness. All speaking characters in a film should have personality. It is rare, though, that they are involved in the causes of major earth-shattering events or their solutions. That's the province of the major characters. When you write your supporting characters, make sure that they don't run the danger of upstaging the protagonist. In your film, the protagonist has to remain the most developed character.

## Extras and Bit Players

Depending on the type and breadth of a film, whether it's a sitting-room farce or a remake of *Gone with the Wind,* the number of actors will obviously vary. The bigger—or more extravagant—the film, the more "extras" will be needed. Extras are those people who provide "background presence," for instance, soldiers getting ready for battle or people walking by in the park. The demarcation line is between those who have lines to say and those who only have screen presence and don't speak.

The scriptwriter is not going to be too concerned about extras. If your protagonist needs to walk through a picket line, all you'll need to write is the description line, something like "HARRY gets out of the cab and walks through the picket line." The director will be in charge of filling in the details. The picket line would be composed of extras, hired on a daily rate.

## Bit Players

Some characters are so minor, they may make a only single appearance in your screenplay. These characters are played by actors who do "bits," thus the title *bit players*. A bit player can deliver lines, and gets paid accordingly. Unless the production is a low-budget flick, where some of the lines are made up as it goes along, the lines spoken by a bit player have to be written.

Look at the minor scene on the opposing page.

If this quick scene makes it to the camera lens, you could bet that the actor playing the cabby is going to make the best of his two lines. (He'd like the director to notice how he was trying.) It has been known to happen that a director has liked a particular actor so much, he asked for another scene to be written for him.

Just because a character comes under the heading of a bit player doesn't mean a scriptwriter should dismiss the part and more or less write in anything just to fill space. Minor though it may be, the writer has the opportunity to make some kind of mark by writing dialogue, for instance, for a waiting cabby who does no more than just say, "Where to, sir?" You may keep this in mind as you write even the most minor characters—your work could start off the career of a small-role actor.

HARRY goes up to a parked cab and taps on its roof.
The CABBY looks half asleep; Harry taps again.

The CABBY opens one eye.

                    CABBY
          What's your problem?


                    HARRY
          Are you for hire?

The CABBY opens both eyes.

                    CABBY
          You could say that.

## Chapter 10

# Conflict and Its Purpose

Conflict is the underlying emotion that sets the pace, creates suspense, and demands a resolution. As such, it is the major element in any screenplay. If there is no conflict, no tension, and no controversy, the audience won't stick around to keep watching the film. No film, no matter how well made, will work without a conflict—whether the conflict is between characters or presented in some other way.

## Understanding Conflict

Pick up any newspaper and you will find reports of immediate conflict. There is no getting away from it; countries have conflicts, as do people. The minute you start thinking about it and look inward, you find your own conflict.

Conflict is the cause of most of the trouble in the world, yours and everyone else's. Therefore, it's no wonder that it's at the heart of the dramatic structure. We all find it easy to recognize when we see it and most people with any sense can feel it coming. Looking at it from that point of view, it should not be too difficult for the scriptwriter to come up with some fine examples.

## The Major Conflict

Any minor conflict is still a conflict, but to drive the story along what you need most is the major conflict, which is most often played out between the leading character and the antagonist. An intrinsic element of conflict is drama; without drama you will not have much in the way of conflict, because for it to manifest requires opposing forces. The two characters have to come up against each other; one option is to set up the plot so that the antagonist wants what the protagonist has—or vice versa. This struggle between the two characters is adequate for serving as the basis for the creation of a major conflict.

"To most people, even those who don't read much, there is something special and vaguely magical about writing, and it is not easy for them to believe that someone they know—someone quite ordinary in many respects—can really do it." —John Gardner

But you don't need to pit two characters against each other to create a major conflict. The antagonistic force doesn't have to be a person. The following are a few examples.

**Animals:** This approach has been in wide use ever since the *Godzilla* movies. More recent examples are *Anaconda* and *Jaws*.

**Natural occurrences:** A tornado, a storm, an earthquake, and other natural disasters can serve to create conflict. For instance, in the film *The Perfect Storm*, the fishermen are pitted against the storm that threatens their lives.

**World events:** Wars, revolutions, even elections all create sources of conflict. In *Saving Private Ryan*, World War II may be seen as the antagonist, or at least the antagonistic setting.

**Things:** Ever heard the expression "man against the machine"? Yes, even objects can serve to create a major conflict. A good example is *The Matrix*. Can you think of any others?

**The self:** Struggles between the protagonist and himself (or herself) are not an uncommon way to create conflict. *Fight Club* is a good example of how you can create a conflict of the self.

**ALERT!**

It's suggested you view *Mississippi Burning,* starring Gene Hackman. It was written by Chris Gerolmo and directed by Alan Parker. Loosely based on fact, it concerns race and tension in the Deep South. It's a good example of identifying the source of conflict, which is not a person or a thing so much as a philosophy.

As you can see, virtually anything could create conflict. Keep in mind, too, that the conflict may very well be internally created; in other words, it is a person's reaction to something that starts things off, not necessarily the action itself. What may get one person riled up may not bother another. This leads us into the area of perception. Imagine how you feel when you're driving and somebody cuts you off. It won't help any if this guy happens to be driving a slick sports car and is chatting on his cellular telephone at the same time. It's doubtful if you'll have the peace of mind to think, "Oh, well, never mind, I've got plenty of time."

If you wish to see conflict at work in literature, it would be a good idea to read the best of Stephen King (or maybe view some films based on his novels). King is a master at creating a combination of conflict with tension and suspense. Of course, he is not alone among writers at doing that.

"The good writing of any age has always been the product of someone's neurosis, and we'd have a mighty dull literature if all the writers that came along were a bunch of happy chuckleheads. Let's face it, writing is hell." —William Styron

It is possible that the idea of major conflict has grown up along with the screenplay formatting of the major plot points, which were created to demonstrate change in the direction of the forward movement of the action. Do not be deceived; if in doubt, take a look at life, maybe your own life. It will be immediately apparent just how many swirling emotional elements there are in just a single day.

## Minor Conflicts

It is very easy to slip into believing that all you need in a screenplay is a single conflict to get things going and to sustain the action for a hundred minutes or so. But that's not true at all, and a far cry from reality. While there may certainly be a single major conflict driving a film, there are always a number of other lesser manifestations.

For example, in a war film the major conflict is the war itself. But another, minor conflict may have to do with a soldier and his girlfriend back home—perhaps she's tired of waiting for her soldier or, on the contrary, the soldier meets a local woman while he's stationed in some foreign country. Surprisingly, in some circumstances one conflict can override another. To that soldier, the conflict with his girlfriend may temporarily become more important than the war.

# A Secondary Conflict

*Shane* is the archetypical Western: A lone cowboy rides into the valley from out of nowhere, solves the problems of the settlers, then leaves the valley slightly the less well for wear, but still triumphant. The major conflict has to do with solving the settlers' problem, but there is a secondary conflict here as well.

In the film, Shane, played by Alan Ladd, stays with a homesteader family called the Starretts. The young son, Joey, played by Brandon de Wilde, looks up to Shane as a hero. The mother, Marion, played by Jean Arthur, is obviously taken with him in her own way. She cautions her son not to become too attached to him (a clue to the audience).

The father, Joe Starrett, and Shane become friends. In the third act, Shane decides to go into town to shoot it out with a professional gunslinger who has been brought in. Joe Starrett wants to go instead of Shane; he says it's his fight. The two men battle it out and Shane wins by knocking Joe unconscious with the butt of his gun. Shane, who is by now obviously in the guise of the other man in Marion's life, has done the right thing by saving her husband. (The audience knows that Shane is faster on the gun than Joe could ever be.) Shane and Marion shake hands, look long and hard at each other, and Shane rides off to the gunfight.

**FACT**

It has been said that *Shane* (1953) reflected America's postwar crisis of identity because it challenged the idealized frontierism and presented a grimmer view of the violence that shaped the West. It developed the theme of the individual at odds with society.

The conflict between Shane and Marion is thus resolved. No harm has been done to the marriage, although the audience knows Marion will always love Shane. They know that because they have seen the setup before, although it may have had a different conclusion. The final conflict is played out between the gunfighter, Palance, and Ladd.

Ladd is faster on the draw but is shot in the back or in his arm by another cowboy; the audience is left not knowing how badly Shane has been hit. Joey, who watched Shane kill Palance and had come to try and stop Shane from leaving, can only watch him ride out of the valley. He calls out after him the well-known words: "Shane. Shane, come back. Bye, Shane." In the classical manner, the ultimate conflicts are resolved at the end of the third act.

# Personal Relationships

On the face of it, it wouldn't seem too much of a stretch to come up with conflict in personal relationships. Many of us would only have to think about our own. One popular type of love conflict is the "boy meets girl, girl meets another boy" plot. But to be good takes a little more thought and imagination than that.

If the writer is working on an adult project, it's a reasonable presumption to conclude that most people in the audience are going to know about personal relationships. What the writer should try to do is to set up a plot line where the audience feels fairly confident about the outcome. To do that, you should use an established scenario the audience is immediately familiar with. Then you fool them.

ESSENTIAL

The characters you create should be put together well enough so that the audience believes in them. One way to approach this is to base your characters on real people. If you steal from real life, your creation will be more likely than not to turn out believable.

## Love-and-Hate Plots

The ultimate conflict involves love and hate, two sides of the same coin. Frequently it is part of a family feud, brother against brother, sister against sister, blood against blood. Elia Kazan's *East of Eden* is based on the novel by John Steinbeck, which in turn is loosely based on the biblical story of Cain and Abel, and it is probably the most well-known "love and hate" plot line. The film was billed as being intense in its emotions and explosive in its passions. It was James Dean's first major motion picture; he played Cal—the bad brother modeled on Cain.

Set in the time of World War I, the story revolves around what would today be termed a dysfunctional relationship between Cal and his brother Aron (Abel, the "good" brother) in the rivalry for their father's affections. The father is of course Adam, played by the then-imposing Raymond Massey. Given some thought, it can be seen that the plot line of the Biblical story could very easily be adapted and brought into current times, which has frequently happened.

Like Steinbeck's *Grapes of Wrath*, which wasn't short of conflict itself, the *Eden* picture was set in the rural area of Salinas, California. What held the audience in *Eden* was wondering how the major conflict would be resolved. Would Cal be reconciled with his father, and what would be the outcome for his brother Aron?

Like many Biblical plots, the Cain and Abel one is a classic. It is safe to say that the Bible, together with the works of William Shakespeare, provide a wonder chest of plot lines, most of them rich in conflict. It wouldn't hurt any aspiring scriptwriter, or even some successful ones, to study both collections.

## Internal and External Conflicts

Conflicts in personal relationships may be a mix of internal and external conflicts. A good example of how that's done is Shakespeare's *Macbeth* (there are two very good film versions: the Orson Welles version of 1948 and the Roman Polanski film of 1971). The murder of Duncan by Macbeth provides great psychological insights: Macbeth's inner turmoil before the murder and his external turmoil with Lady Macbeth both before and after it.

**FACT**

The audience is thrilled at the way the hero combats and overcomes all the conflicts that are thrown at him. They sit enthralled, just like the audiences before them who sat watching those old-time cliffhanger serials.

Films that concern themselves with brother/brother, sister/sister, and sister/brother relationships provide good movie fodder. Here are a few other examples:

- *The Brothers Karamazov*
- *The Fabulous Baker Boys*
- *The Krays*
- *A River Runs Through It*

- *Rumble Fish*
- *True Confessions*
- *Duel in the Sun*

# Conflict Resolution

It is agreed that conflict is an essential ingredient of a dramatic work. Without it, the story is not going to be able to hold an audience. The word in the film industry has gained tremendous cachet, but, in doing so, a question has arisen: Has the weight of the word depleted the subtleties in a script or just become another overused word?

Going to war is an issue of conflict and a creator of suspense: Will the lover/husband/wife come home and when? A divorce is the same, as is a trial for murder. But is missing the bus and being mad at the driver who wouldn't wait an issue? The answer must be relative to the individual. To a person with a short fuse it might well be an issue, a conflict, but not to Forrest Gump, to whom life was like a box of chocolates.

The scriptwriter has to tread a narrow causeway, one that goes between the dictates of the industry and the creativity of the artist. In many ways what is called a conflict is sometimes more of a mystery. If a character is late for an appointment, and the reason hasn't been given to the audience either verbally or visually, then that is a mystery to the audience. Creating mystery is good because it makes for involvement by the audience; they have a need to know the answer to the question, Why was he or she late?

## Providing Clues Along the Way

It's probably not a good idea to keep the audience hanging around too much before they are at least given a clue as to the answer of a mystery. The clue, when it is given, should be just enough to pique their interest, such as, for instance, when the wife discovers under the front seat of her husband's automobile the cheap brooch that doesn't belong to her. What "sells" the answer is that the audience has seen that brooch on the "other woman" at an office party, as they know the wife must have.

**ALERT!**

Even if you have seen *The Godfather*, it is suggested you view it again. Francis Ford Coppola and Mario Puzo received Oscars for the screenplay, and it also won the Best Picture award.

In addition to conflict and issue, there's another word that might be considered: question. That is, question in the minds of the audience, not in a character in the film. Again, posing questions in the minds of the audience is an excellent involvement device. Will the hero catch his flight? Will his wife dump him? Will it rain on his parade?

It's therefore not a bad idea for a scriptwriter to arm himself or herself with a battery of these devices, all of which are designed to involve the audience: conflict, mystery, questions. They can be used either separately or together and might be brought out when the writer needs to create a plot point, either major or minor, or to heighten the attention of the audience for dramatic purposes. Keep them in your device arsenal.

## The Conflict in *Loophole*

To end the chapter on developing conflict, let's take a look at how conflict plays out in the film *Loophole*. In this particular case, the conflict is between people and an institution—the bank, or the bank vault. Here is a group of criminals headed by the arch-thief, Mike Daniels, and aided by a regular citizen, Stephen Booker. They are planning to rob a London bank vault by going through the sewer system and up through the floor of the vault.

The scriptwriter sets up the problem, creating a story that's concerned with a group. The attraction is to develop a group made up of a wide variety of characters. The problem is not to create a cliché group of thugs. Research is required so that the writer finds out that many professional thieves are family men, people you would be very happy to invite to the block barbecue.

The sort of film in the past that worked well with a group was *Stalag 17* with William Holden. Set in a POW camp, it was very successful and considered to be the forerunner of the television hit *Hogan's Heroes*. Of course, there have been many war films that were poor examples of a group depiction; audiences frequently even saw the same actors in more or less identical parts in different productions.

**QUESTION?**

**How do I write convincing group characters?**
As the writer has no control over casting, the best that can be done is to provide fascinating descriptions of characters, in addition to writing great dialogue for them. You want someone in casting to say, "We gotta get somebody great to play this guy."

## Secondary Conflict

Still in the first act of *Loophole*, a meeting is set up between Daniels and Booker in a park. The purpose is for Daniels to sell Booker on coming in with him on the robbery. Booker's problem is his wife's reaction to him being out of work without any money coming in. This has resulted in Booker driving a cab for cash and incidentally meeting Daniels. Thus, Booker has a dual conflict: the problem with money and his wife and reconciling to becoming a thief.

Of course, Booker joins the thieves and Daniels presents him with an immediate cash influx; in the short run, his conflicts are solved. The secondary Booker conflict provides the film with a parallel story line that involves the middle-class poor. There are other problems, including the discovery by one of the thieves that he has a heavy case of claustrophobia going down manholes into sewers. Another member develops a nasty problem with rats. Ⓔ

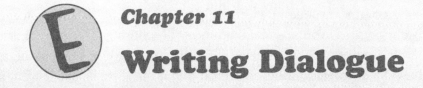

*Chapter 11*

# Writing Dialogue

Now that you've considered your protagonist as well as other characters, it's time to put them together and make them talk. The dialogue in movies is there not only to fulfill a function of the plot and to inform the audience but also to assist in moving the story line forward. In other words, it keeps the film in motion.

# Getting the Basics Down

Dialogue in movies should contribute to the forward motion of the film. It is important that stress be laid on the use of active verbs. Verbs are strong words. Look at some of the great passages in film and you'll find a surprising number of active verbs in them that indicate action and reaction.

Study common speech patterns and when you use them, try for consistency, unless you are making fun of the character. For example: "Yes, well, I entered Saks, perused the fashions, made my selection, and purchased a garment." Another person might put it this way: "I went into Saks, took a look at the dresses, and bought one."

When you write the dialogue, avoid clichés, like the following gems:

- "It's quiet—too quiet."
- "I've been blind—blind, I tell you."
- "Oh, my God."
- "You look like you've seen a ghost."
- "Get your act together."

**ESSENTIAL**

Just because a writer isn't aware of who may be uttering the words in a script doesn't mean there should be any less effort behind their composition. The choice of the words to be said is the scriptwriter's responsibility. It should be taken very seriously.

The problem with clichés and avoiding them is that with audiences they feel cozy, they are so familiar with them. After all, clichés were once phrases that worked very well in particular situations—so well, they were repeated over and over again until they gained their present status as trite and overused expressions.

One way to avoid being blatant is to preface the statement with "I know this is a cliché, but . . . ." The trouble with that is that it's becoming a cliché itself. However, if you create characters who are witty and bright, then chances are you won't get yourself involved in cliché hell.

# The Reality of Cinematic Dialogue

When you are watching a movie, the conversations you hear onscreen sound pretty realistic. But if you were to compare them with a real-life conversations, you'd realize that most of the time they're not so realisitic. Real conversations have hesitations and repetitions. They break off and start up again, there are sudden shifts in topic, and often the speakers will go off-tangent and then forget what they were trying to say in the first place. It is rare that movies will tolerate real dialogue—it would seem unrealistic. Movie dialogue has to be custom-made.

The trick to writing movie language is that while it is not like real language, it has to sound as if it is. This means that it ends up being more focused, more to the point, and less rambling. The utterances are shorter and monologues are discouraged. In many ways the language looks as if someone went through it on the page and did an editing job, which they probably did.

## Movie Influence

There are theories that movies affect society so much that people emulate them. There's been little doubt that fashion in movies has affected fashions in the marketplace. Behavior, too, is influenced by the movies, as well as television—particularly in teenagers. The same goes for speech; people say things the way they are said in movies. It is often difficult to know which came first, the real thing or the movie version.

**FACT**

There is no grammar to worry about in dialogue, because very few of us use correct grammar when we speak. The chances are that if we did, we'd sound very pompous. Here's a well-known example from Sir Winston Churchill: "This is something up with which I shall not put."

Slang comes and goes and frequently originates in movies. Automobile sales are even influenced by films, the obvious example being the Aston Martin in the old Bond films. (Apparently they've changed brands to BMW.) The Mustang used in *Bullitt* not only gave the manufacturer some great exposure but provided the movie business with a lesson in how to film fantastic car chases; the one in *Bullitt* was shot on the hills of San Francisco and has ever since been endlessly copied.

## Direct, Quick, and to the Point

The general principle of good writing, that of using the active instead of the passive voice, is absolutely suited to writing for the movies. The active is more direct and vigorous than the passive. Writing in the active mode uses fewer words to say the same thing as in the passive: Mack was fired by Grant (passive); Grant fired Mack (active).

At the same time, you need to be as clear as possible. As some people in the business like to point out, writing a screenplay is not like writing a book. When we read, we always have the opportunity to go back and reread something we don't get the first time. But when you're in a movie theater watching a film, you can't just rewind and see the scene again. In a sense, there's only one first time in movies—the words are said, then they're gone.

**ALERT!**

Even if you've seen the film before, please take the time to rent *The Maltese Falcon,* John Huston's first film as a director; he also wrote the script. It's a marvelous example of sharp, taut dialogue, plus some great characterizations. Incidentally, this was the third, and the best, version of the same story.

Returning to the spec script formatting, it is almost the rule today that scenes shouldn't run to more than two or three pages, two to three minutes. (Compare that to scripts from decades ago, where a scene that took up eight to ten pages wasn't a surprise.) The answer, of course, is to break the long scene down into smaller segments, and if you find any of your characters with a long speech, break it up into shorter ones. The other device is to interrupt the scene with cutaways. This means the camera cuts away to, say, a woman in the crowd weeping. (Many directors make a point of routinely shooting cutaways, which can frequently get them out of an editing hole. They do the same with close-ups.)

# Writing in the Vernacular

All professions have their own vernacular. If you happen to be at a cocktail party for computer programming nerds, the odds are you might think you're in China for all you could understand of the conversation. When you create a character who is a computer programmer or a hacker, you'd better bone up on the computer vernacular, or that character is not going to ring true. You don't have to know a lot—just enough to convince the viewer of the character's authenticity.

## The Vernacular of Class

As we all know, there is a vernacular of the social orders and it is in place throughout the world in one guise or another. Another way to put it might be to say that there is a pecking order wherever you go. For the purposes of looking at how this pecking order affects a screenplay and the characters in it, let's presume our illustration is the United States. Most people who have traveled in the United States are aware of how in many ways it is a continent made up of fifty countries—if not more.

**FACT**

If you are writing a part that requires a dialect, don't worry about it. If the character is an Irishman, for instance, you'll have identified him early on. If you start trying to be clever and writing phonetic spellings with all the apostrophes, you will get yourself into deep trouble. Just sprinkle the odd Irish phrase around. The actor will fill the rest in very nicely.

Each "country" has its own history of development and it even has its own particular laws. Certainly there is a wonderful selection of accents and ways of speaking. It follows that if you people your screenplay with a variety of characters from across the country, they must exhibit the many facets of their origins. The point of all this is that you should check yourself to be certain that not all the people in your script speak and act in the same way.

# Telephone Conversations

Telephone conversations can be handled in a number of ways. First, you have to decide who is calling whom, then the purpose of the call and its emotional thrust, if any. There must be some reason the caller feels he or she needs to contact the other person. Today you have additional options: land line or cellular call?

If the call is made from a cellular unit, does some kind of urgency prompt making it that way, or is it purely convenience? If the caller doesn't want the call—at least her side of it—to be overheard, then obviously she'll choose a suitable location, perhaps a moving vehicle or in the park, while taking a walk. Is the person being called available, or is there an answering machine and message?

## The Unseen Listener

If you decide your telephone scene will show only one of the characters, then you have to create a one-way conversation. Do not presume that you will be able to get away with the audience being able to hear the answers of the character on the other end of the phone. (Not so with an answering machine, of course.) Enter into writing the scene knowing that you have to provide a one-way conversation from which the audience will be able to intuit what the unseen/unheard character answers.

A good way to research how you should write this kind of one-way conversation is to eavesdrop on one of those cellular conversations people make in closed areas like bookstores, buses, trains, or in the theater.

If you do end up wanting to show both parties having a conversation, each time the camera shifts from one person to the other, you'll have to set it as a different scene, alternating between the two. So one conversation will be set up as a series of scenes.

Get into the habit of reading your work from the point of view of what you can cut. Ask yourself how you can get your scene over in seconds instead of minutes. Test for yourself just how long three minutes is. Time yourself to see how many words you can deliver in a minute. You'll be surprised.

## On or Off Camera?

The 1959 film *Pillow Talk* with Doris Day and Rock Hudson is a romantic comedy that revolves around the two leads sharing a telephone party line. Naturally, they talk to each other without making a call; when they pick up their receivers to make a call, they find the other party has done the same, and so they end up talking to each other. Thus, the comedy form of the film title is established.

The point is that the film uses a split screen, Doris in one half, Rock in the other; they are both in their respective beds. It's a technique rarely used today, although in 1968 *The Thomas Crown Affair* with Steve McQueen and Faye Dunaway used multiple, virtually fragmented split screens. You, the writer, have to make these decisions: Do you want to show both parties or only one of them? If you decide on one only, which one—the one making the call, or the one receiving it?

## The Line or Scene Everyone Remembers

You can write good dialogue, or you can try your hand at great dialogue and write lines that will be remembered and that your audiences will quote for years to come. *Casablanca* gave us a wonderfully written scene by the Epstein twins: Captain Renault and Rick (Claude Rains and Humphrey Bogart) are in conversation, and Renault is speculating on what brought Rick to Casablanca. Rick's answer is his health: "I came to Casablanca for the waters." Renault is surprised: "Waters? What waters? We are in a desert." Rick's answer is typically short and caustic: "I was misinformed." That is a scene everyone who has seen the picture remembers.

Many films have produced a line or a scene that instantly identifies the film. Ask anyone for the scene they remember most from *Butch Cassidy and the Sundance Kid.* Ask them which picture is famous for its shower. Even a single line can become part of the language. "Go ahead, make my day," uttered by Clint Eastwood's character Dirty Harry, is an example.

At the very end of *Some Like It Hot,* Jerry (played by Jack Lemmon), who had been masquerading as a woman, is in the boat of a rich suitor, played by Joe E. Brown. The suitor proposes, and Jerry then tells him he's a man. There's a pregnant pause, and then the suitor retorts, "Well, nobody's perfect." Only three words, and it is one of the great last lines in a movie.

Some of these one-liners are so entrenched that it's not necessary to give more than a clue for instant recognition: Clark Gable as Rhett Butler to Vivian Leigh: "Frankly . . ." And what about another one-liner from *Casablanca*: "Round up the usual suspects."

**FACT**

They used to say about the great writer Paddy Chayefsky *(Marty, Network)* that his dialogue sounded like it had been tape-recorded. That annoyed Chayefsky, who would reply, "The whole labor of writing is to make it look like it just came off the top of your head."

## The Dazzle

How do those very special words and scenes come to be? Very often out of the blue, and probably more by luck than design. The writer is likely to be reaching for something—he or she doesn't know what it is, only that something is missing. Maybe it's just a couple of words, or one scene.

The motivating force behind all that is almost always a problem that needs to be solved. Writers shouldn't get nervous about problems—in fact, problems to be overcome very often lead to better results. Suddenly the idea comes and when it's written down on paper, the writer will look at the words on the page and—*zappo*—realize how right they are. Ⓔ

## Chapter 12

# Valuable Writing Techniques

There is an art to learning what to write—but it's equally important to know what you should hold back. Less can be more. In a way, by writing too much it is possible to insult the audience. They may not know they've been insulted, but what they will know is that they are getting bored in a hurry and perhaps they need to go out for some more popcorn.

# Avoid the Exposition Ditch

Exposition is "telling" or explaining as opposed to showing. At its best, exposition is done at the beginning of the film, where it is most acceptable. At its worst, exposition is having two characters tell each other information that, logically, they should already know. For instance, let's say a couple is swapping gossip about two of their mutual friends. But the whole point of the conversation is merely to clue in the audience about those two people, who may be introduced later. So, let's say Joan and Bill are having coffee. Joan says, "Did you hear that lovely Laverne is pregnant?" Bill replies, "Yeah, that's rotten. I guess that bastard Sam is the father." As you can see, this is too obvious of a ploy—not a good idea.

The audience has been "told" that the lady Laverne is lovely and that Sam is a bastard and that the latter made the former pregnant. A number of years ago on the stage, exposition had become mechanical and unrealistic. Think of dear Agatha and her mystery plays/films for instance. In the same way as Laverne and Bill, a maid and a butler might come on-stage to talk about the main character, who had yet to appear, and end up telling each other things that logically they both would already know.

ALERT!

Take a look at *Diner.* There are some good examples of exposition being used in a creative way, often with humor and bickering between the characters. In this film, the audience has the opportunity to learn about the background of the characters without being told about them.

## Show, Don't Tell

Instead of relying heavily on exposition, what the writer should do is provide visual clues, which allow the audience to compose the picture as a whole for themselves. It is highly probable that even with the small collection of clues from the first scene, the audience would almost immediately be trying to figure out what's going on in the film and what the story is going to be about. What should be avoided is the temptation to "tell" the audience by, for instance, writing in dialogue for one of the characters that, instead of providing clues, explains by lengthy exposition what the back story is about. When that happens, it is the writer being slack by taking the easy way out.

Let's look at an example of how information is conveyed to the audience without the use of exposition. The film is again *Shane*. In the opening sequence, Shane (played by Alan Ladd) rides into the valley behind the opening credits and meets the boy playing with his toy gun on the Starrett homestead. In the sequence, Shane is startled by the boy and almost goes for his gun. The boy's mother and father don't turn to each other and whisper, "That man's a gunfighter."

We all know why they didn't, because the scriptwriter knew his audience was educated in the way of films and that they didn't need any prompting. Shane is a lone rider, he's dressed like a gunfighter, he moves like one, and he doesn't say very much. Conclusion: Gunfighter.

It's also almost a certainty that we don't need to know about Shane's background, because most movie gunfighters have a murky one. In any event, that part of the character's back story emerges gradually as the film progresses—the best way for exposition to work.

**ESSENTIAL**

Exposition can be communicated by dialogue, a monologue, via action, or by costume, sets, light, and sound. The most heavily relied-upon tool for such communication is the dialogue, but make sure this is done realistically. Otherwise, the whole exercise will sound phony. Subtlety is the key.

# Relying on Metaphors and Symbols

Another way of communicating meaning is by relying on symbols and metaphors—literary devices that work by way of comparison. How does this work? Let's take a look at an example. You've got a scene with Gertie and Adam, and Gertie wants to convey to Adam that she remembers the time they were lovers.

INT. A SUPERMARKET    NIGHT


ADAM has a shopping basket. GERTIE, a shopping cart.
They are both standing by the bakery section.


                    GERTIE
          Been a long time, Adam.


                    ADAM
          Yeah.


    GERTIE looks into his basket. She sees cereal, bread,
a frozen dinner, and some dog food.


    ADAM glances into her packed shopping cart and sees a
variety of baby food containers on top of other
groceries. He looks at GERTIE and smiles.


    Adam goes to reach for a packet of cookies. As he does,
he touches Gertie's hand as she goes for the same brand.
    They both laugh.


                    GERTIE
          Arrowroot, remember?

You might note that with very few expository words, combined with a selection of props, the audience will have deduced a fair amount of information. Obviously, Gertie has at least one child; it would seem Adam lives alone with a dog. The audience gathers that when they were together, they used to eat arrowroot cookies. In a way, the cookies are a symbol for their togetherness.

At that point, the audience will be trying to figure out if there is any future for the two of them. That will be relative to how much they already know about the couple and their current status. Whatever that might be, the fact that there will be a question in the minds of the audience is a plus; they are involved. The essence of good exposition is grounded in the technique of holding back as much as you can.

**Do you always need exposition, and if so, why?**
Generally you do, one way or another, because the audience has a need to know about the characters and their backgrounds. One way to give them that information is by exposition.

**QUESTION?**

# Using Flashbacks and Voice-Overs

While the classical method of handling exposition is to create a conversation and have it take place in a location that adds interest, there are other methods as well. Using flashbacks and voice-overs are two methods that require a fair amount of talent to pull off. In addition, they are not exactly considered to be of high priority by the people who read scripts in Hollywood. We have all seen these methods in action in movies.

Flashbacks in the old days could often be predicted. The actor would turn to his beloved, perhaps, and say, "It was a long time ago, my love. Things were very different then, we were very different." At that point there would be a DISSOLVE and probably some romantic background music, and the film would take the audience back in time.

Voice-over narration is most often used as the unseen voice of a speaker comments on the events the audience sees on the screen. It is also used to explain something that hasn't been shown visually or to complement images that require further explanation.

**FACT**

If you listen to the Hollywood experts, you will be told to create conflict at every turn. Imagine ways to pit your characters against each other, they say. The theory is that the more conflict the better. Be that as it may, mother's advice might be appropriate: "Everything in moderation, dear."

## A Newsreel

*Citizen Kane* uses both techniques within the device of a newsreel being shown in a projection room. This is early on in the picture, immediately after the Rosebud sequence with the glass ball and Kane's deathbed shot. It is obvious that we are watching a newsreel that has been compiled to illustrate Kane's career. A *News on the March* title comes up and a man's voice starts the voice-over narration.

As the newsreel ends, the lights come up in the projection room. A discussion takes place about the newsreel and it is decided that another angle is needed that tells not only what Kane did but also who he was. On that premise the picture proper begins, as a reporter starts his investigation.

The newsreel technique, which is very effective, would today, of course, be done by a simulated television news program. And, as has been done in other pictures, it would quite probably use real-life commercial news anchors. The point here is that this kind of production device can add tremendously to the verisimilitude of the picture.

## Moving the Story Forward

In *Sunset Boulevard* (1950), flashbacks and voice-over narration are used to tell the story. The film stars William Holden as Joe Gillis and silent-screen star Gloria Swanson as Norma Desmond. German film director Erich von Stroheim plays Norma Desmond's valet/chauffeur and former husband. It was written by Charles Brackett, Billy Wilder, and D. M. Marshman, Jr. The picture received rave reviews and Wilder won an Academy Award for Best Story and Best Screenplay.

Wilder took a big gamble in that he had the picture open at the end of the story and used the voice of Gillis, who is dead, to narrate the film, more or less start to finish (or perhaps it should be said, from finish to finish). The original start was of shots of Gillis in the morgue talking, voice-over, of course, to the other bodies in the morgue. The bodies answer back and explain how they got there. Apparently preview audiences were so put off by the sequence that it was cut.

**ALERT!**

It might be a good idea to get hold of a copy of *Sunset Boulevard* to view and study. It is a masterful picture and well worth the pleasure. You might also consider buying a copy of the screenplay.

The final cut version opens with a close-up shot of a street sign, *Sunset Boulevard,* stenciled on a curbstone. Police sirens are heard and policemen and newspaper reporters are seen crowding around a disused swimming pool. There is a body floating facedown in the pool. A man's voice is heard: "Yes, this is Sunset Boulevard, Los Angeles, California. It's about five o'clock in the morning . . ." The voice is that of William Holden. He starts to tell how he got to be dead in the pool.

The shot changes to show a view of Hollywood and some apartments. The voice-over continues and tells what he used to be, a scriptwriter, where he was living, and that he wasn't doing too well. There is another shot change to the interior of an apartment. It's not very spacious nor affluent looking. Joe Gillis is sitting on the edge of a pullout bed typing. The doorbell sounds.

At that point the story/film starts its new chronological order. Gillis gets up and opens the door. Two men have come to repossess his car. After some chitchat the two men leave. The voice-over starts up again to explain what is going on in his life, which isn't too much. Gillis picks up his car, which has been parked in a back lot. He goes to Paramount Studios; all the time the voice-over continues telling the audience what's going on.

We are now into the picture proper and while there are a few more incidents of voice-over sequences, the film then proceeds. The technique reappears whenever it's necessary to fill the audience in on what's in Gillis's mind. This continues right to more or less the very end with Gillis back in the pool floating facedown. In spite of the production technique being totally illogical—a dead man telling how he got that way—the film was a tremendous critical and box-office success.

**ESSENTIAL**

If you intend to use the devices of flashbacks and/or voice-over, you had better be sure the person you are going to submit your script to is the accommodating sort. It would be an advantage if you knew him or her fairly well before you submitted your script.

## "Telegraphing" What Comes Next

Telegraphing means exactly that, letting the audience know what's coming next instead of holding it back. For example: The boys are in the saloon and the topic of conversation is about the hero and what to do with him. The sheriff is down at the other end of the bar and can hear the conversation. The villain leans into the group and says, "I'd give a mighty sum to whoever takes care of that problem."

The sheriff looks into the gigantic mirror at the back of the bar. He sees this runt of a cowpoke. He is hitching up his pants. He looks around at nobody in particular. "Hope you all heard what I said," the villain says. The runt turns and walks slowly out of the saloon. The sheriff watches him in the mirror. The villain looks up at the mirror. His eyes lock with the sheriff's. Guess what? You're probably dead right.

### The Tenor

Let's try another scene, the outside of a theater. There is a notice up that says: Auditions—Tenors Only. Inside the theater a tenor is finishing his audition; he is thanked and leaves the stage. There are a few people in the front stalls. Everyone is very well dressed and all seem very pleased with themselves. The musicians talk among themselves.

A small group of men are discussing the merits of the tenors who have auditioned. They are obviously the nobs of the theater. Some shake their heads. A cleaning woman with her mop approaches them; she hangs around on the fringe. She tugs on the sleeve of one of the men and says, "Excuse me, sir." She has a broken English/Italian accent.

> **ALERT!** Don't use flashbacks or dreams to fill a segment. Remember, the audience has had a movie education and will recognize anything that doesn't have emotional or dramatic weight. It is not a deficiency for a scriptwriter to have originality.

She seems to know the man, and they have a lively talk. The man turns to his companions as if to ask their forgiveness. The man turns back to the woman, nods his head, and she beckons into the darkness. A young man appears; he is poorly dressed but holds himself well. He goes up onto the stage.

The young man acknowledges the group of men and the conductor. He leans over the orchestra pit and says something to the conductor. The music starts; it is Puccini's *Nessun dorma!* from *Turandot*. The music swells and the sound of a wonderful voice comes from the young man. His mother (the cleaning woman) is weeping with joy.

## Cliché-Ridden Scenes

It's doubtful if we could get more cliché-ridden than those two episodes. Nevertheless, perhaps some even had a lump in the throat in the second example. Everyone, of course, knew what was coming, not only because they had seen something similar before but also because they were pitched to the lowest sentimental common denominator. If you are ever tempted to write in that manner, try to restrain yourself.

As everything has happened, particularly in the movies, it is not always easy to critique yourself, especially if you are writing to a deadline. Nevertheless, try to find strong words to use to create strong scenes. Remember, it is not so much the subject of what you write, but the style in which you write it. Look at each scene you write as an individual challenge, even though the scene is part of many others.

> **Here's a list of some redundancies you should do without:** absolute necessity, conclusive proof, invited guest, past history, old adage, free gift, future occurrence, and final outcome.

As it is unlikely that you will be the director of the film, the best bet you have to infuse something new into the production is via dialogue. Dialogue has a built-in reputation for being difficult to write. There are writers in Hollywood who write only dialogue; that's all they are paid to do. Try to see that doesn't happen with your script. It doesn't have to.

## Elements of Suspense and Tension

Holding back is an important contribution to the creation of suspense, for it is always the threat of something happening that causes the trouble. The saying "We have nothing to fear but fear itself" is absolutely true. Therefore, you should try to withhold as many clues as you can before revealing the monster, whatever or whoever that may be.

Every writing teacher under the sun will virtually bludgeon their students into the ground trying to convince them that it is far better to show than it is to tell. As far as a movie script is concerned, particularly as it's a visual medium, following this maxim is imperative. Try to keep the telling to an absolute minimum. Audiences can be quick to pick up the meanings behind what is implied visually.

> **What exactly is tension?**
> It's a state of anxiety that is induced in the audience by the threat of danger to a character. Tension increases as the action increases and decreases as it reaches the denouement. You can increase or decrease the tension by manipulating the time between the two.

## The Value of Silence

Silence is the ally of tension and suspense; couple it with controlled time and you can create high tension. Time elongates and contracts itself on film, and this is something the scriptwriter can take advantage of. To become acclimatized to screen time, run a couple of tests for yourself. Rent some suspense pictures—*Psycho* would be one good choice—and watch them on your VCR with a watch that has a second hand and some notepaper handy (if you have one, a stopwatch would be perfect). Be prepared to stop and rewind segments.

Find the sequence in *Psycho* where the private detective goes into the house late at night in an effort to talk to the mother, the scene where he starts going up the stairs. Now get ready to time that sequence. Time the silence from the beginning of the shot up to the point where the musical effect tells us that Mother with her knife is coming. Analyze the scene and the emotions it generates.

Figure out how it works and what part silence has in contributing to the tension. When you get ready to do this, keep in mind that Hitchcock was a master of this kind of emotional manipulation. You couldn't have a much better tutor. In fact, you could emulate what some famous directors have done by going through the list of Hitchcock thrillers and spending your spare time studying them. It will be time well spent.

## Test It Out

Try this test on yourself just to get the feel of how time is not as constant as we think it is. This should enable you to rethink the concept of time when you have no control over its passage. Again, get your stopwatch and paper. Go to the television; the evening news is a good time. Just as the anchor says something like "We'll be right back after these messages," start your stopwatch and record the time until the anchor is back.

Get ready to do the same thing again, only this time when the anchor tells you about the upcoming messages hit your mute button and start the watch. You will be surprised how the time changes when your brain isn't occupied actually listening to the advertisements, only watching them. They say of the great play/scriptwriter Harold Pinter that he had mastered the art of writing the silences.

## Tension in *Double Indemnity*

Tension is a subject that can be neither overstressed nor overdone. To illustrate, let's look at one of the motion pictures you have already been advised to view: *Double Indemnity* (1944). It was written by Billy Wilder and Raymond Chandler and directed by Wilder. It is based on the book by James M. Cain.

The story line concerns a plan to commit an elaborate insurance fraud. It is to be carried out by an insurance agent, Walter Neff (Fred MacMurray), and the wife of the victim, Phyllis Dietrichson (Barbara Stanwyck). Their antagonist is the insurance company investigator, Barton Keyes (Edward G. Robinson). The audience knows Neff is going to commit the crime; the fascination is how and will he get away with it.

Early in the first act, Neff calls at the Dietrichson home to talk over insurance with Mr. Dietrichson, who happens to be out. Phyllis Dietrichson interviews Neff dressed in a bathrobe; she says she's been sunbathing. She's wearing an ankle bracelet, which is deliberately featured by Wilder. What follows is some wonderful dialogue, no doubt written by Raymond Chandler, who was a master of the cynical innuendo. By the end, it's clear that Phyllis and Neff will become an item.

**FACT**

*Double Indemnity* is considered one of the top film noir pictures of the 1940s. Film noir came out of the Depression era and was born in the hard-boiled fiction of Raymond Chandler and others like him, the films of Hitchcock and the actors like Robert Mitchum. As the name suggests, film noir films were always shot in black and white with high contrast lighting.

The tension/suspense is built into the picture because the audience knows the intention. Now they are going to watch as it's carried out. However, this is given even greater emphasis by Wilder, who changed the opening of Cain's book by structuring the progression in more or less the same manner as he did later in *Sunset Boulevard* (1950)—a flashback to the crime, except this time it's the villain and not the victim who is doing the talking.

# Involving the Viewer

If a film does not involve the viewer, which frequently happens in the second act, the audience will become bored and some even might leave the cinema. For a look at a film that manages to involve the viewer, we can return to *Double Indemnity.* In the second act of that picture, the Dietrichson murder is to be carried out in the victim's car and is a classic example of holding back and showing. Mr. and Mrs. Dietrichson leave their house and drive off on the way to the local train station, where Mr. Dietrichson is scheduled to catch a train to his class reunion. Phyllis is driving; her husband broke his left leg at work and it is in a cast. The tension has been built already because Neff and Phyllis have planned in advance that Neff would get into their garage and hide himself in the back of the car.

Conflict is used between people and events to tell stories that reflect the problems between adversaries. It is best if the resolutions do not come about until the end of the scene or the picture.

Much of the reasoning behind these actions is covered with voice-over commentary from Neff's dictation. The script structure is wonderful, with shots of Neff cowering in the back, his view of the heads of the Dietrichsons, close shots of Phyllis, and all the while regular chitchat between the couple in the front seats. As the car reaches a dark street, also prearranged, the shot is on Phyllis's face, which shows acute tension. She hits the car horn three times: again, a prearranged signal. Dietrichson is speaking and his voice suddenly breaks off and dies into a muffled groan.

The actual murder takes place off camera, as it concentrates on a close-up of Phyllis's face. The only sounds are of struggling and the dull sound of something breaking. The reaction Stanwyck's face portrays as her character listens to the murder of her husband is considered a mastery of acting. Phyllis drives on, her teeth clenched, her eyes staring straight ahead.

Without giving away the resolution entirely, the picture ends at dawn in Neff's office. Keyes has shown up and the police and ambulance are on their way. Overall, the film is a prime example of a superbly sustained production of intense tension and suspense. It merits considerable study by any ambitious screenwriter.

## Chapter 13

E

# Auditory Cues in Writing

We have spent quite a bit of time paying attention to the visual cues that must be present in a screenplay to make it work. But, as was said before, the screenwriter is dealing with the auditory just as much as the visual. Beyond the most obvious auditory component—the speech of the dialogues—what other factors should the screenwriter pay attention to? This chapter will examine some of the auditory factors that make up a great screenplay.

# The Educated Audience

Such is the power of movies that many young people know more about how movies and television programs play out than they do about current events, geography, and a number of other topics previously thought to be common knowledge. Modern audiences are watching films in greater numbers than ever before, not only in the cinemas, but also on television, videotapes, and DVDs. In the process, they have become educated as to what to expect from films. Dating from somewhere around the introduction of MTV and its frenetic crosscutting, the technique of speed editing found its way into film production and strongly influenced the way modern films are made. As a result, we've got what might be called the "short attention span" audience.

If films from the 1970s back to the 1930s are viewed and compared with the modern product range, it becomes very apparent that dialogue has been on the slide. There's not so much of it around anymore. Some of this may be the lack of good writers, but more likely it is due to the increase of action combined with a lack of acceptance by a younger audience for all that talk. In the field of comedy, humor has similarly changed from the clever, witty, and subtle to the more obvious.

Of course, everything has its cycle and there is a hint of new directions. It is generally agreed that when the cycle of change returns to its roots there is a fair chance films will re-emerge improved. The insistence on cutting away elaborate verbosity in screenplays, and thus from the subsequent productions made from them, seems to show that there are improvements afoot.

## Seeing Characters Think

At the same time that verbosity declines, there is a marked return to the camera lingering on a character, generally in close-up, in order to indicate thought. It was said not so long ago that you could tell what Brando was thinking by looking at the back of his neck. Another way of putting this is to say that there appears to be a movement toward creating greater depth of character, as opposed to cardboard cutout characters where action is taken without apparent prior thought.

**ALERT!**

Anytime there is the beginning of change in the air, it offers opportunities for the energetic and talented to take advantage of it. This is no more so than in the field of entertainment. It is the wise artist who monitors the changes going on around him or her.

## The Elements of Holding Back

Writers are learning that because film audiences know about movies, there is no need to send messages ahead to tell them what's on its way; these messages can be either verbal or visual. For instance, in the old days the setup might be an urchin hanging about and a posh business-type coming out of his house. He is wearing a blue pinstripe suit and a bowler hat, and he carries a briefcase.

The urchin has a banana that he starts to peel. The posh man keeps coming, his nose in the air. The urchin is eating the banana. Still the businessman keeps coming. The urchin throws the banana peel over his shoulder and walks off. The posh man doesn't see the banana. He steps on it, his legs go from under him, and he ends up on his rear end. (Predictable result: Audience laughs.)

Today, because audiences are film-educated, all that is needed are the setup and four shots: Posh man comes out of his house. Urchin is eating a banana. Urchin walks away. Posh man's legs go out from under him and he lands on his rear end. (Predictable result: Audience laughs.) The audience has filled in what wasn't there. You don't have to show all the details.

## Paying Attention to Sound

A screenwriter must think beyond physical images and words to be spoken. Just as audiences will vary considerably in their opinions about a picture up on the screen, so a reader in an office evaluating screenplays will, in principle, be doing the same thing to the pages on a desk.

Most of the sound heard coming from a film in a cinema appears to be real; much of it isn't, and even if it is, it is frequently manipulated.

The majority of the sound recorded on location will have to be re-created and rerecorded in the studio, then eventually mixed with all the other sound tracks: dialogue, music, ambient sound, and so on.

**FACT**

There are sounds in modern productions that don't exist until a film goes into production. For instance, in *Return of the Jedi,* which is part of the *Star Wars* trilogy, a laser gun might be fired. The sound had to be invented, and now appears in the sound library, to be used in other movies.

## Indicating Sounds

The text on the pages has to conjure up pictures in action complete with sounds. Writing a script to format means it is necessary to type in block caps the important actions and sounds. Remember that included in the list of people who will need a copy of your script are the sound technicians; they have to come up with the sounds.

When you write direct indications of important actions and sounds, you can set them in all caps, which is rather like using a colored marker pen over certain words to bring them to the attention of the reader. However, it's very important that you don't get carried away to the point of writing a whole slew of ambient sounds in caps: he SNIFFED, she CLEARED her throat; the script readers and even the sound tech would go crazy reading the script. A rule of thumb might be that the sound should have some dramatic import to warrant caps. Always remember that the sounds should have a direct relevance to character and place.

### Getting Attention

Obviously, sound effects play a major part in the film. Sounds in movies are manipulated so well that the viewer gets heavily involved in listening very carefully to the picture. Below are a few examples of sounds and actions that should be in CAPS so that the words catch the attention of the sound technician. A sound or action put into caps has to have a value that demands its caps.

- The door SLAMS shut.
- The wheels of the car SCREECH.
- JAZZ music is coming from . . .
- He SHOOTS him dead.
- Everyone is SHOUTING.
- The door slowly SQUEAKS open.
- He CRASHES into the garbage cans.
- His trousers RIP.

Imagine a scene in the studio where a character is waiting for a telephone call. Now, don't think that the director is going to have a real phone on the set that someone off camera will call. The scene will be the character sitting at his desk, shifting papers around; on cue he looks at the prop telephone receiver, ponders, then picks it up and starts talking; nobody on the set hears the phone ring. That'll be put in later by the sound tech. And it will be just the right kind of ring at just the right volume. However, as far as the scriptwriter is concerned, type: The phone RINGS.

How do scriptwriters deal with overlapping dialogue and/or sounds? They may use ellipses ( . . . ) to indicate an interruption, or at the beginning of an utterance to indicate partial dialogue as it comes into earshot. You could indicate the device by writing: START SOUND MONTAGE. You would subsequently have to write: END SOUND MONTAGE.

## Using Music As Background

There is another way in which sounds can be used either in conjunction with words or without them: music. It's good to add music into your screenplay, as long as you are careful. The screenwriter should never write in the name of a song or of a particular artist. However, you can indicate a type of music coming from a CD player or a television, for instance, by writing: A LOVE SONG PLAYS.

Background music is not in the domain of the screenwriter, although the composer may well pick up emotional cues from the script, or more likely from viewing the film in the editing process, and subsequently back it with an appropriate score. You may have played your favorite sentimental love song in the background when you wrote, but that's where it should stay. If you write with the idea in the back of your mind of how dramatically the scene is going to play when it's backed by Tchaikovsky's *1812 Overture,* forget it.

It is suggested that you get a copy of *Blow Out.* The screenplay was written by Brian De Palma. De Palma also directed the film, which stars John Travolta. The story of *Blow Out* is about a soundman.

## Sounds and Suspense

You can think of sounds in a similar way that you would think of music. (It may not have escaped you that music is sound, although to some it's noise.) Say you have written that your protagonist, Zack, is in a room at the top of the stairs. It is night and a single bedside light illuminates the room. Zack is looking for something and is opening and searching through drawers in a chest.

Then you write in the description and sound: "Zack starts and looks up. A RUSTLING comes. Zack turns to the door. The RUSTLING fades. He turns back to a closed drawer and slowly opens it. The RUSTLING comes again." You can play with the sequence of rustling and turns until you get the rhythm the way you want, which should be building tight tension. If you want to get really melodramatic, you might risk writing in that the light flickers.

## Using Props

You can use sounds to communicate information. But there's another way of cluing in the audience about what's going on: using props. Props are any objects used by the actors as they enact their scenes. One popular prop in recent times is a cellular phone. It's versatile because it can communicate any number of things—whether the person is a businessman or a social butterfly, for instance.

**FACT**

Props are often used as "business," an old vaudeville expression used by comics that refers to filler material (or props), perhaps used to distract the audience or change their attention from one thing to another.

Notice how often you have watched a scene that was interrupted by a telephone call. Telephones can take on a personality or act as a metaphor. For instance, every time something bad is going to happen in the film, the phone rings just before it does happen. Do that a couple of times and the audience will have absorbed the significance; some may even jump in their seats the next time the phone rings up there on the screen.

## Avoiding Exposition

A prop used as a piece of business can get you over an endless need to explain. You want to avoid too much explanation in the form of dialogue, because it very often leads to a film being dragged forward instead of moving at a reasonable clip. The business of explaining is actually exposition, which means some background information needs to be told. It generally takes place at the beginning of the movie.

Unfortunately, exposition is frequently mechanical and unrealistic, not to mention boring. If at all possible, try to find a way around it. A flashback is one way to avoid exposition, because you can go back in time and show the information as it happens. A conversation between two characters is another, which also gives you the opportunity for some humor. And using a prop may work, too. Ⓔ

*Chapter 14*

# A Screenwriter's Discipline

You may think that a screenwriter's job is full of glamour and excitement—sipping cappuccinos at a café as you type away at your laptop and send off the screenplays to your agent and on to the final sale by the biggest Hollywood studio. But even if you are that successful, writing is a grueling undertaking, and you need to develop some discipline and a good ethic in order to persevere.

# Time to Work

Without any discipline, a writer is not going to get far. It is not true that you can sit at the keyboard and channel Orson Welles. You actually have to work. Once you start this writing game, you will develop a rhythm to your day. If you have the luxury of choosing any part of the day or night to write, think about your style and your personality. Are you a morning person or a night person? Do you need structure and discipline to move forward with a project, or are you more easygoing—you always get the job done, but you don't follow any rules?

**ALERT!**

Remember, you are in charge of your schedule. As long as you set up a good time to work, it doesn't matter whether it's in the middle of the night, early in the morning, or in the late afternoon. What matters is that you have a set amount of hours during which you expect to get some work done.

## Make the Time to Write

Even with the busiest schedule, you can still carve out hours of time for writing. Some writers find they can do their best work only at a certain time of day; others learn that they can start their engines whenever a free hour surfaces. Some of these authors establish a certain number of hours each day that they must ply their craft. Others determine that they must write a certain number of words or pages at each session. Through writing you'll settle on your own best schedule and writing-output goals. But you have to put in the time to find your answer.

If your life is already filled with career, family, volunteer work, and extracurricular activities, you can still find time to write. It may be hard, but you can do it. Consider getting up a bit earlier than you usually do, if you're a morning person. Night-lifers will find it easier to head to the writing table after dinner or after everyone else has gone to bed. Instead of going out to lunch every day, just about everyone can brown-bag it, close the office door (or go to the library or a park), and set aside that time to write.

On weekends, try setting aside a bigger block of time to create. Think about enlisting friends or family members who might be able to take over chores for you or who you might be able to trade services with. You can also hire a baby-sitter, dog walker, gardener, or such to free up some time for you to write; the expense may be high, but the cost to you of not writing may be higher. By sitting down and really studying what you do and when you do it, you'll likely find some daily time that you can dedicate to your craft.

## Developing a Writer's Routine

It's important to create a sense of routine. In some writers, this borders on superstition. For instance, some people will use only a certain kind of pencil for writing. Others won't begin until they've got their favorite coffee mug filled with coffee. Even if you're working at home, you can create a certain sense of work time, as if you are actually leaving your home and going to the office. This kind of routine contributes to a writer's well-being and helps her or him to feel comfortable with the creative process.

Keep a log of your work, where you note how many pages you've done each day as well as how many pages you are hoping to complete by specific dates. These logs are great for creating a sense of commitment to the work you need to do and a sense of accomplishment over meeting your goals.

## Set up Your Workplace

In many authors' experience, surroundings and equipment that suit their personalities and styles make it more likely that the blank page before them will eventually be covered with compelling writing. In fact, the ideal writing place may automatically, just by your being there, set your writing muscles in motion.

What would work for you if you had the luxury of setting up a custom workplace? Think about how you like to read or study, how sound affects you, how easily you're distracted, how disciplined you are, if you need people around you, and your general nature.

It will work well, if you have the space, to set aside part of where you live in which to work. Tell everyone, particularly children and animals, to keep away and not to touch anything, under fear of retribution. (Always number your pages.) If it's possible, leave your working pages out on the table; don't be overly tidy. Then in the morning, eyes open, coffee cup in hand, dressing gown tied, drift by the table.

You will typically look down at the odd page or two and something will catch your eye. That's when you do an edit. At night, or whenever you decide to stop work, take some advice from Mr. Hemingway: "Always stop when you know what comes next." If you do that the odds are you will never get what some people call "writer's block"—running out of what to say.

**FACT**

You need a place where you can write comfortably and where your materials will be safe from prying eyes, jelly-dripping fingers (except your own, of course), and constant interruption.

## Developing a Style

Because making a motion picture is such a collaborative business, it would seem unlikely that different styles could emerge. And yet, there are some films that are so distinctive, you can name the writer without referring to the credit list. Sooner or later, a good craftsman will develop a style. A style can only be experienced, learned, or copied—it can't be taught.

Taken to the extreme, some actors develop a style that they reproduce in every film they do. When that happens, it is said that they have become typecast. A distinctive style is also seen in the work of many directors, with the most obvious example being Alfred Hitchcock.

In filmmaking these days, the power is overwhelmingly in the hands of the directors. So, for a writer to develop a distinctive style, it is probably wise to work toward having a style that is aimed at appealing to directors. Thus, a certain director may like your particular style and seek you out for his or her next production. As time goes by, your style will then stand a chance of being recognized, at least in the business if not with the public.

## The Signature Piece

Every now and then a film or even a certain scene will register so forcefully with an audience that it becomes what is called a signature piece. Orson Welles, for example, did that in a film called *Touch of Evil* (1958), which he wrote (adapted would be a better word) and directed. The film subsequently underwent a series of editing changes until it was almost what is often called a "director's cut."

**QUESTION?**

**What is a director's cut?**
Director's cuts come about when, usually some time after the original release, the director is able to persuade the producers to have the picture recut. That usually means restoring footage the producers had cut.

The signature part of the film is the opening scene, a wonderful three-minute shot that covers four blocks of a seedy Mexican border town with the sound of a ticking bomb mechanism in the background. Naturally, this eventually leads to an explosion. The scene has become part of cinema folklore and joined a group of film excerpts that aficionados treasure.

## How It's Done

All signature pieces were written or came to be written in a variety of ways, some out of a casual conversation, perhaps, some from the urgency of time when the scene was needed in a hurry; others were meticulously planned.

It is often a case of happenstance; a writer or director doesn't start out saying, "I'm going to write a fantastic scene." It just seems to come out that way, and in retrospect the writer often says that the scene just seemed to come without much in the way of effort.

The image of the writer sitting at his or her desk tapping away on a keyboard, while true, is not the be-all and end-all of how a script gets to be not only written but put into production. The writer who is at the beginning of a career should learn quickly that an open mind is an essential. This means a mind that is prepared to be surprised by the unexpected and to profit from it.

Every writer of merit in whatever medium, every serious scientist, every painter of high regard, all of them would sound like an echo of one another if they had to answer the question: "What is the secret to your success?" Some would smile before they answered because they knew from experience they wouldn't be believed. "Simplicity," they would say. "The elegance of simplicity."

## Consider Collaboration

You may have heard people say that writing is a solitary craft. However, sometimes people work best as collaborating partners. In a way, writing with a collaborator is like being in a marriage. The fact that only half of all marriages seem to work out shows that collaborating isn't always an easy undertaking. It goes without saying that the collaborative couple has to be artistically compatible.

Where it does seem to work best is with comic writers. Often they work together in the same room, where they can play the jokes off each other. One will come up with an idea and the companion will bounce back with a line, and so it goes on. Note that they are not necessarily writing with some implement; they are talking out loud to each other, then writing the results down.

Probably the two most dramatic collaborators were Orson Welles and Herman Mankiewicz, who between them produced the screenplay to *Citizen Kane.* The two men met in New York City and worked together with John Houseman and the Mercury Theater's "Campbell Playhouse" radio shows. The stories surrounding who wrote what and when of the original screenplay for *Citizen Kane* are virtually endless. What isn't in doubt, however, is the critical success of their product.

## The Magic of Billy Wilder

It was three other men whose collaboration produced a virtually endless list of wonderful pictures. The writer and director Billy Wilder led this group. In 1942 Wilder began collaborating with another writer, Charles Brackett, in their work at Paramount Studios. Together, the two men produced *The Lost Weekend* and *Sunset Boulevard*, both of which earned Oscars for best screenplay. After *Boulevard* Wilder left the partnership and took up with another writer, I.A.L. Diamond. Together they produced *The Apartment*, which won Oscars for best picture, director, and screenplay. Both men were also responsible for *Some Like It Hot*. Billy Wilder was probably the last of the major writer/directors to come out of Hollywood; twenty-five major films list Wilder as the director and cowriter. In his later years, into his nineties, he continued to go to his small office in Beverly Hills to work.

**ALERT!**

Collaboration can come about because each member has a certain talent that balances out what the other has to offer. Each person brings all that he or she is to a work, whether it's a film, a book, a painting—their prejudices, loves, and hates. Often, bringing together different viewpoints, personalities, and passions leads to a more well-rounded final product.

# Participate in a Writer's Group

If collaboration is not really for you, you may still benefit from participating in a writers' group for screenwriters or a more informal network of friends who are also working on writing screenplays. As you progress through your work, you'll definitely need to bounce your ideas off other people—your potential audiences—and having a supportive group that will give you constructive criticism can be very helpful.

## A Critical Approach

There is another and very important advantage to having a well-run writing/reading group. Essentially, you will be forming the classical workshop. Not only is the purpose for you to read your stuff and get objective opinions, it is for you, and all the others, to learn from being a critic yourselves.

**FACT**

After attending a creative writing class at Iowa University, Flannery O'Connor said she didn't learn very much except when she was given the opportunity to review the work of others. It was then, when her mind was given over to concentrating on other people's work, that she learned about writing.

To be a good critic you have to concentrate on the work; when you find something that you think needs attention in someone else's work, you are automatically drawn to wonder if you have the same problem in your own writing. So this whole operation works both ways for all. Don't take every little piece of criticism to heart. Take what you need and move on.

## Chapter 15

# Revising Your Work

Almost every writer of merit revises his or her work. Writing bad first drafts is not a sign of ineptitude, and there is no reason to feel guilty. On the contrary, don't ever expect to sit down, write something, and send it out. In fact, many writers spend more time rewriting than writing. Did you know that Hemingway rewrote the end to *A Farewell to Arms* thirty-seven times?

## It's an Essential Step

You are creating a work that you might think of as your baby. You've sweated over it on your own. You know what it's like to be a writer facing a blank screen or a blank piece of paper. Maybe a year has gone by and at last you have the 120 pages of your final draft stacked in front of you. And someone is telling you it needs work? Listen to them, maybe it does. Put the draft aside and go fishing for a day or two. Think about your possible career in the screenwriting business. Come home and think again about the advice. After all, it is your first screenplay.

Everyone works in a different manner; one way to deal with the necessity of editing is to give yourself some distance from the script. When you finally reach the finish line, don't write FADE TO BLACK and then turn the pages back to FADE IN on the same day. Take a break; go shopping—hey, chop wood in the rain if that's what it takes. In fact, do anything but rewriting that script. It is important that you try to get some time and distance before you go back and reread your work.

**ALERT!**

Remember: The first draft of anything is just that, a first draft. Now you have to start doing the real work. In scriptwriting it is estimated that three scripts have to be completed before you know what you are doing. This may be one reason why many people don't make it in the business.

## The Power of Rewriting

To improve your first draft, you will need to rewrite. Your motive during this process must be to make your screenplay better. Know in advance that there are going to be weaknesses in your work. If in doubt, ask yourself how many Oscars you have to your credit.

It's a very good idea to have a strong element of humility toward your work. If you need inspiration, view any of the finest movies you can rent and study their screenplays. Try to pick out the scenes that really stun you, then ask yourself, how did they do it? Then look for your own weaknesses in your script; find what doesn't work. Look at every scene that doesn't move the story or a character development forward. When you find it, cut it; learn to be ruthless.

If you can't see your scenes visually, something is wrong. Don't write the words so they "tell" the reader/viewer what is going on; the words have to be employed in "showing" what is happening.

Let's take a look at an example. Your description line could read: "Jason looks at the candle. It goes out. He stands back against the wall. His hand moves to his holster. The door creaks and moves, as if to open. Jason pulls out his gun and cocks it." This kind of writing shows what is going on, and from the action we can infer what is happening inside the character as well. He's cautious, perhaps scared, and he's ready for action. Read the passage again. Does it help you visualize what is going on?

**ESSENTIAL**

As you should know by now, Hollywood pundits advise that everyone should write three screenplays before they even think of sending one out. They say it's going to take that long just to get the hang of it. It's just not likely that you will hit the movie jackpot with your first effort.

## How Film Editing Relates to Written Editing

In literature and journalism, "editing" is the process of rewriting, but in film it's the editing of the 35mm film—it used to be that the editing process meant cutting and gluing together pieces of film. That's why "editing" in film isn't used to refer to the process of rewriting. Instead, the script drafts are known as *rewrites*.

However, both rewriting and editing have more in common than might first be thought. It all depends on when the function is done. If you are writing a spec script, then the rewriting is probably going to be done before almost anyone else sees the finished product. The editing of a film typically takes place when the shooting and tampering with the script are over.

And, of course, there are times when someone in power orders up retakes or the scripting and shooting of new scenes in an effort to either improve or save a film. A general clue, incidentally, as to whether or not a film has been in trouble is the number of screenwriting credits on the finished product. If you see three or more writers credited, it's a fair chance something was wrong; of course, often the writers brought in to "doctor" a script aren't credited. (This doesn't necessarily apply to a comedy, where groups of writers are often used.)

**ALERT!**

It would be a good idea to get hold of a copy of *The Good, the Bad, and the Ugly*. This is a Clint Eastwood "Man with No Name" picture. What you should be studying is the sparseness of the dialogue. Consider whether lack of dialogue detracts from your understanding of what is going on, or whether it adds something to the picture.

Never become so cynical that you believe that once your spec script has been bought, it will immediately go out for rewrites by some other writer and so there's no need to bother doing rewrites yourself. Grasp the principle that subjectivity reigns, which means that much of the rewriting by others is aimed not at improvement but at change. This change is to suit the opinion of someone else. There are people out there who would change anything just to put their seal on it.

## A Life of Its Own

It is true that when you are engaged in writing a book or a screenplay, the project takes on a life of its own. Well, you might have to tame some of the vicissitudes that have crept in. Be very suspect of what you may have written in the evenings, with a glass of red wine at your elbow to bolster you and some romantic classical music on the stereo; the result is probably junk. It may be a nice idea to think that good things come from a bottle, and they certainly do, but not when you are serious about your writing.

Try to leave your editing work out on an open table with a pencil or two close by. Leave being tidy to other things. It will happen that in the early morning, cup of coffee in hand, eyes nearly open, that you will pass the table and won't be able to stop taking a look at the open pages on it. Your eyes will somehow be drawn to a line of dialogue. "Ah," you say, and make an edit.

## The Rewriting Process

When you sit down at your keyboard or typewriter, you should not only be trying to come up with some decent words, you should also be seeing (visualizing) in your mind's eye what the words are supposed to mean. It's a theory that the reason why so many Hollywood scripts are not up to par is that the writers were looking out at the beautiful Pacific Ocean from their Malibu decks when they were writing them; try looking at a blank wall.

Let's presume you have achieved a reasonable amount of objectivity about your script. You know what it is supposed to do and how. You first check the structure, making sure that the three acts, plot points, and such, are in the right places and do their job. When you started out writing the screenplay, you had a very good idea in mind what it was you wanted to accomplish. Now that you've reached the end, it's time to go back and check to see if you have achieved your original purpose. It's not unlikely that your purpose got lost along the way—if that's the case, don't get discouraged. Instead, try to figure out ways of how best to fix this problem.

## If in Doubt, Just Cut

Probably the most difficult part of rewriting is deciding on what has to go. After all, it's your baby that's being considered; you have sweated for hours over its prose, dialogue, and images, and now, you wonder in dismay, something has to be cut? Why, you might ask, is it necessary to consider cutting? Perhaps your script runs to 140 pages, so at least twenty of those have to end up in the trashcan.

But there are other reasons as well. It could be that your second act is too slow, or that the transition from the first to second act just doesn't work. Or it may be that a secondary character is just not working and you need to consider cutting him out completely, and possibly replacing those scenes with something else. Whatever the case may be, you have to sit down and make some hard decisions.

**FACT**

Paddy Chayefsky was a marvelous playwright and screenwriter: *Marty, The Hospital, The Goddess,* and *Network* are just some examples of his work. He had this advice about editing: "First cut out all the beautiful stuff, slash, slash, slash." What he meant was that what the writer thinks is beautiful is ego, and it should go.

## The Importance of Intuition

As you make cuts, consider something called intuition—your intuition. It is said that the more you rely on it, the stronger it will become. Look at it from this point of view: You read over your pages and you suddenly get a gut feeling; that's your intuition. When what you have just read over doesn't seem to scan quite right and something seems wrong with it, generally your gut feeling is right—there is something wrong with it.

Once you start cutting, you'll feel like a weight has been lifted from your shoulders. If you are worried about cutting, always remember that you can save your original files or copies and can always go back to them if you don't like your changes. Nothing will be gone for good, unless you don't save the old versions.

## Reviewing Your Dialogue

A problem that can come about in writing dialogue is being able to tell if it plays, meaning if it works. An actor may often turn from a page of script and say, "It doesn't play." What this means is that either the rhythm is off in some way or that some of the words are not easy to pronounce. (Steve McQueen, who was not well educated, had that difficulty.)

Reading over your own work to evaluate it is never easy, and this is especially true when it comes to reading dialogue. One method you might adopt is to record your dialogue on a portable tape recorder and play it back to yourself. Try to give yourself some distance from the time you made the recording to the time you listen to it—that'll help with your objectivity. Ask yourself: How does it sound? Is it right for the characters? Does it sound like them? Is the dialogue "written on the line," which means, does it say what it means?

If you are lucky enough to have a companion or friend who is interested in what you're trying to accomplish and willing to get involved, then you might see if they would read the lines with you and maybe even act them out. If you have kids and the film is not inappropriate for their reading, you may want to have them re-enact your scenes—they'll enjoy it just as much as you will!

# Get a Second Opinion

Showing your first draft around in a cozy writing group may seem like a good idea, and it is—until you suddenly find some of your smart dialogue being read back to you from someone else's script. One method that can work is to read and play out your script to a moviegoing friend. Pick a friend who likes the kind of films that are close to what you've written. In other words, perhaps don't risk your high-energy murder mystery on a person who thinks *The Sound of Music* was the greatest film they've ever seen.

Before casting your pearls around, first take a good hard look at your proposed recipient. Let's say you have already established that they like your kind of movie. But, what else might be a factor in their opinion? Well, their gender, for one: There are boy films just as there are girl films.

## Be Aware of the Risks

There's a very good reason for going to all this trouble finding the right audience for your first draft. It's called rejection. Rejection, as you must know, is someone telling you that your wonderful screenplay is not quite what he or she is looking for. The fact that this person probably didn't know what he or she was looking for in the first place has nothing to do with it.

**What if the person who reads my script hates it?**
Ask the reader why she hates it and to justify her opinion. Then listen; you might very well learn something from an objective reader. It doesn't matter so much that the reader hates it; it does matter that it generated an emotional response.

The worst response you can get from your friendly reader is something like this: "Oh, I thought it was very interesting." Forget it, it's all over. If your objective movie reader thinks what you wrote was very interesting, move on. What you do need is this: "Gosh, this was fantastic, great, I loved it." Now you might be in business. The blah opinions and all their justifications will kill you, both emotionally and practically.

## Save Your Work

The last—but certainly not least—piece of advice for this chapter is to save your work. When you've got your first draft, save it, and use a copy file to start on your revisions. Throughout the process, you may decide that the revision just doesn't work and go back to the original draft to start over. If you don't keep track of the changes you've made, it's going to be very difficult to retrace your steps, and you may be tempted to give up.

Plus, saving your work in this day and age of computers is just plain common sense. Save your work and date it. If you don't want to overload your computer, save it on a floppy disk, ZIP disk, or CD-ROM—whatever you have available. Some people even go through the trouble of keeping their backup disks in a lead-lined safety-deposit box. (Lead-lined is not a joke; ask your bank about it, most are lined that way.) One last note: You can lose data from a disk if you leave it next to a vacuum cleaner that happens to be switched on. Ⓔ

## Chapter 16

# Adaptation from Another Work

A film adaptation means that instead of inventing the story yourself, you adapt it from another genre—most often a novel or a short story. Other genres that have been adapted for the silver screen include the comic strip, video game, opera, musical, and many others. To write an adaptation you have to have the rights to do so. Some works are in the public domain. For all others, you need to get the permission of the copyright holder, who may hire you or sell you the movie rights.

# Consider Writing an Adaptation

It has been estimated that well over half of all feature-length films made since 1920 have been based on plays or novels. This doesn't mean there are few ideas around; more often than not, the reason behind adaptation has been to try and capitalize on the advance success of the forerunner. And yet, the most frequent complaint about book adaptations is, "It wasn't as good as the book."

**FACT**

Here is what Thornton Wilder had to say about adaptation: "I do borrow from other writers, shamelessly. I can only say in my defense, like the woman brought before the judge on a charge of kleptomania, 'I do steal; but, Your Honor, only from the very best stores.'"

Adaptation is so popular, there is an Academy Award category for screenplays based on material previously produced or published. Here are a few examples of screenwriters who have won the Oscar in this category:

**1999:** John Irving, *The Cider House Rules*
**1998:** Bill Condon: *Gods and Monsters*
**1997:** Brian Helgeland: *L.A. Confidential*
**1996:** Billy Bob Thornton: *Sling Blade*
**1995:** Emma Thompson: *Sense and Sensibility*
**1994:** Eric Roth: *Forrest Gump*
**1993:** Steven Zaillian: *Schindler's List*
**1992:** Ruth Prawer Jhabvala: *Howards End*
**1991:** Ted Tally: *The Silence of the Lambs*
**1990:** Michael Blake: *Dances with Wolves*

For those who might be serious about adaptations, it would be a good idea to perhaps dig out a couple of original works that became films and compare them to the way in which the adaptations were accomplished. Be warned, there's quite a selection to pick from; about 85 percent of all Oscar-winning best pictures are adaptations. You will probably find that many of the adaptations were successful because the adaptor didn't slavishly follow the original.

## Hard Look at Adaptation

Adaptations come about for a variety of reasons. The two main ones are: One, the original has established a tremendous success in its own field, for example, the *Harry Potter* books; and, two, Hollywood is so short of good story ideas, they frequently fall back on adapting someone else's successful brainstorm. In many ways it is an unexpressed concession to the need for a good idea, which shows the high value good story ideas have in the movie business.

ALERT!

Every time you look at a film from now on, be sure to check the screenwriting credit. There will be times when you might be surprised at the source. Films have been based on newspaper articles, songs, poems, real-life experiences, and almost anything else that provides the core of an idea.

However, it's very important to understand that it is not going to be an easy job. In the first place, whatever work you choose to adapt has been created in an entirely different medium, and adapting it for the screen will require you to make changes that may inadvertently affect the intent or quality of the work. Of course, some works are much more easily adapted for the movies. There may be some truth in the assertion that author Michael Crichton writes his books as extended film treatments, thus making them simpler to adapt. Have you read *Jurassic Park*? If so, you may have noticed that it reads just like a movie. However, that's not usually the case with most novels.

In many ways, adapting an idea is simpler than doing the same to a novel, short story, or play. For instance, if you were going to work on trying to convert a novel to the screen that was written by a famous contemporary author, you might find working in his or her shadow not only intimidating but also daunting. Adapting the works of authors long dead might be a better bet, except that the really good ones will be in short supply, having already been adapted as films.

## Consider the Logistics

You will also need to consider the time period and the set requirements needed for the work you plan to adapt into a screenplay. If the original you are working with deals with a time long past, the director will have difficulty getting together the set, costumes, and other props, so you may diminish your chances for selling the screenplay to a studio. After all, the budget of turning a screenplay into a film is on the agenda of all film producers, and the writer is asked to keep that in mind when structuring the movie version of the book.

Fortunately, you do have flexibility in adapting works for the screen. You can actually keep the same story but switch the action into the present, or set it at a different time or location. Think of the inventive adaptation of Shakespeare's *Romeo and Juliet* (1996) by Craig Pierce and Baz Luhrmann.

**ESSENTIAL**

Remember that problems can be good to have because they should be the spur to creativity. Smooth sailing, particularly on a movie, is asking too much anyway; it's very unlikely to happen. The writer may learn to welcome the sudden appearance of a problem because it could well bring its own answer with it.

Millions of dollars are going to be spent on the adaptation, and the producer will be well aware that some adaptations do not automatically translate well to the silver screen and, as a result, bomb at the box office. *The Bonfire of the Vanities* is one good example of how a successful novel was made into an unsuccessful film.

As a scriptwriter you will be aware that extensive location setups for the purpose of getting one scene may not be good economics. Perhaps that scene can be done without or shifted elsewhere, saving some budget dollars.

## Beware of Copyright Issues

The first problem to be solved in adaptation is the issue of copyright. It is not a good idea to write an adaptation in the hope that the owner of the rights is going to be so pleased that he or she will be forever grateful to you. What the owner of the material will be doing is talking to a lawyer. Put another way, it is impractical, not to say a waste of time, to decide to write an adaptation just because you happen to love the subject matter of an original published work.

The only exception to the rule of getting the rights is if the work you choose to adapt is in the public domain—that is, the copyright has expired and no person or estate holds the rights to the work, or the work was created before copyright laws existed (for example, the works of Shakespeare). In this case, you'll be free to adapt the work in any way you like (of course, you'll still need to give credit to the original author). The best examples of works in the public domain quite often adapted for the movies are the plays written by William Shakespeare. Think just how many times his works have been adapted, both successfully and unsuccessfully, for films. In fact, why not rent two or three different productions of the same film and then compare how they were adapted for the screen?

**FACT**

View any of the films made from the books of John Grisham, like *The Client*. Grisham is one author about whom it's said the films of his books are better than the books themselves. That's because they are plot-driven and the structure is uncluttered. As books they are page-turners; as films they are straight entertainment.

## Adapting a Novel

One of the most popular objects of adaptation is the novel. There's plenty of material in a novel to serve as a plot and story of a film. In fact, you are going to have the opposite problem—there'll be a lot of condensing to do. The issue of length is important—remember that you have to aim for a screenplay of about 120 pages.

Putting that to one side, you also have to look at the time frame of the novel you are working with. Does it cover, for instance, a few centuries, or perhaps just forty or fifty years, or even less? A time frame of a generation or more obviously presents aging concerns for the cast and the makeup department.

## Stick to Bare Essentials

Most novels run to around 125,000 words or thereabouts, which means at least 250 pages and up. Something has to go; the eternal question in the adaptation game is, what? The best way to approach the problem is not to fret about what to cut, but to decide what is essential. This comes down to analyzing exactly what the novel is about and what its purpose is.

Try to identify the major elements in the novel; these should include the protagonist, antagonist, and major secondary characters and their value to the progression of the story. What is the conflict and which chapters/scenes contain conflict development? Look at the structure and mark off the three acts. Go right through the book to the climax. Be absolutely certain that you identify the climax and its resolution.

**ALERT!**

Pick up any decent novel you are familiar with and try to decide its purpose. Once you've done that, find out what you could cut without destroying the whole point of the novel. If you have been hired to adapt the novel, these questions will have come up in the prescript meetings, so you will have a set of guidelines already in place.

Pay particular attention to the second act. You may remember the points already made about the second act in a film often being the weakest. Well, the same frequently happens in a novel. That being the case, it will be the second act where you might be able to do your finest cutting.

## What to Leave Out

One first step is to reduce the number of characters or perhaps combine two of them into one. It is well known that in *Gone with the Wind*, which was based on a fairly long book, many characters were either cut altogether or merged into a single one. Try to end up with four strong characters. You will find that the extra characters are often involved in a subplot. Look closely; perhaps the subplot isn't essential to the major point of the story and could be dropped altogether.

## Prose and Show

Some novelists are prone to extravagant prose with long descriptions of characters and places. Others seem to love to "tell" the reader what their characters are feeling. All of this being in love with words can be a bonus to the adaptor. As we all know, words are not vital in a medium where "showing" is the name of the game.

An example: The novelist may write a paragraph describing a magnificent sunset, and some may even get carried away with more verbosity. This is a gift to the movie adaptor, because a few words can cover the same ground: EXT. A SUNSET – DAY. As much as a page of the novel has been converted to one line in the script.

**ESSENTIAL**

A main point of concern when it comes to adaptation is taking what has been expressed in words and achieving the same intent in a visual setting. One way this can be accomplished is by using the voice-over device. Just be sure there is a very good, justifiable reason for doing it.

## Adapting a Short Story

Working with a short story, newspaper article, or another piece of writing of similar length, you've got the opposite problem—the original work may not have sufficient depth and girth to sustain a feature-length film without expansion. That means you are going to have to add on to the work as you adapt it into a script. Sometimes this proves to be so difficult, more than a few studios have bought the rights to a short story only to end up using the title and coming up with an entirely different story for the screenplay. The bulk of the picture becomes the creation of the scriptwriter.

## Adapting from Hemingway

A good example of a short story that needed fleshing out was Hemingway's "The Killers," considered to be one of his finest works. In book form it is just over nine pages long. Typical of the classical short story, it takes place over a matter of hours and more or less in one place, in one small town.

The story opens as two men come into a diner. George, the proprietor, asks them what they want; a young man, Nick Adams, watches the encounter. The men are tough and belligerent; very soon they have taken over the diner. The two men tell the others that they have come to kill a man called Ole Andreson (the Swede).

They say they know he comes into the diner every night. They tie up the cook and young man and instruct George to tell anyone who comes in that they are closed. First one customer, then another, comes in; they leave. Andreson doesn't show up, so the two thugs leave.

George unties the other two. Nick says he'll go and see Ole Andreson and warn him. Nick goes to the rooming house and sees Andreson, who used to be a prizefighter. Nick tells Ole about the two men and that they said they were going to kill him.

Andreson acts as if he doesn't care. Nick asks him why he doesn't get out of town and Ole says he's had it "with all that running around." He tells Nick he "got in wrong" and there's nothing he can do about it. Finally, he says that after a while he'll make up his mind and go out.

The story ends with Nick Adams back in the diner telling George what happened when he went to see Ole. Nick asks George what he thinks Ole did and George says, "Double-crossed somebody. That's what they kill them for." Hemingway's comment on the human condition is in the last line when George answers Nick, who has said he can't stand thinking about Ole. "Well," said George, "you better not think about it."

**FACT**

Hemingway's comments on Hollywood based on the films that were made from his books weren't exactly complimentary. He said the best way to deal with film people was to go to the California state line, exchange your book for the money, then drive like hell back the way you came. Apparently, *The Killers* (1964) was his favorite adaptation.

## The Padding

*The Killers* was made twice as a film, the first time in 1946 with Burt Lancaster and Ava Gardner, then in 1964, featuring Ronald Reagan in his last role before politics took over his life. The lead character in that version was played by Lee Marvin. The 1964 adaptation was originally intended as a movie for television, but it was then considered too violent; times have changed.

In both versions the opening segment was based almost entirely on Hemingway's short story. It was considered to be the most effective part of both films. It's interesting that what was created by the adaptors was overshadowed by the originating short story; the 1946 film was the closest to the original, even down to the dialogue. Try to rent both versions and compare them. Which one do you think works better?

## Adapting a Play

As we all know, plays are usually restricted to interior sets in a theater. This makes them difficult to adapt for the screen. The common device is "opening them out," meaning finding reasons to be on location so that the film version doesn't look like a play caught on film. Flashbacks are often used to give a back story to what wasn't deemed appropriate in the theatrical original. In the theater, reality isn't nearly as paramount as it is in film; therefore, the plays that imply realism often fare better in adaptation.

Some plays can gain immeasurably in film by adding tremendous scope to the restricted play format. The numerous adaptations of Shakespeare's plays serve as a good example of this: *Hamlet* has been adapted eight times, the most impressive of which is considered to be Grigori Kozintsev's 1964 version. Then there is *Henry V* and Laurence Olivier's 1944 production, which demonstrates the one big film advantage with the full staging of the Battle of Agincourt.

**What's the point of learning how to adapt plays?**
Primarily, it's another method of learning about the structure of screenplays. Even if you never adapt a play, and the odds are you probably won't, seeing how it has been done can be invaluable because it makes you think and study.

## How to Retain the Original Concept

The presumption always is that the reason a producer/studio bought the rights to an original property, whether it's a novel, short story, or another type of work, was because of its excellent story line, the author's great literary abilities, and fascinating characters. If you are handed an assignment to adapt a work for the screen, then you have to take a good study of the property.

Your first thought should be: How do you adapt this work but still manage to keep the essence of it? What is its theme, which is what should be the driving force of the story line? If you look back to the *Loophole* example, which was originally written as a novel, it is obvious that the theme is robbing a bank vault that everyone said couldn't be robbed. Everything else in the story is subservient to that theme.

If you were doing the adaptation of the novel *Loophole*, it would be a fairly easy job because the theme is self-evident. But it's not always that way; sometimes you have to dig to find it. Remember that film moves faster than the written word. A book might take eighty pages to introduce a theme; you have to do the same thing in a couple of pages of script.

**FACT**

Written works have the luxury of spending time giving information, providing emotional feelings to convey motives, and including detailed descriptions of whatever the author wishes to describe. The adaptor has to figure out ways to get the same information to the audience.

## "The Book Was Better Than the Film" Syndrome

Why is it that moviegoers can so often be heard saying these words as they come out of a cinema after watching a film based on a highly successful book: "It wasn't as good as the book." What went wrong? Why is it that audiences are always complaining about adaptations?

The reason is probably because audiences think the filmmakers just took the book as is and turned it into a film. They have no concept of the problems and logistics involved. In a way, why should they? If the producers make a film based on another work, why should their problems be mitigating circumstances for what the audience considers a poor job?

**ESSENTIAL**

Relatively few authors turn out to be good scriptwriters. The most famous author-turned-scriptwriter, of course, was F. Scott Fitzgerald. And he wasn't that bad, it was just that he was drinking rather a lot at the time. Writing a novel is very different from writing a screenplay, but both strive for the same result: to reach their reader or their audience.

There is one good reason for the book/film problem: When people read a book, they bring all that they are to it, everything—their prejudices, hopes, fears, background, the lot. So along comes a move studio and makes a film of "their" book. How dare they cast Tom Cruise without asking, when the reader had visualized the main character as Tom Hanks? The readers form their own interpretations and visualizations of a book, then movie people step on their toes when they do something else in the film.

## As Good As the Book

However, there are some adaptations that were successful with the film audiences. *To Kill a Mockingbird* is Harper Lee's only novel, for which she won the 1960 Pulitzer Prize. In fact, librarians across the country have given the book the highest honor by voting it the best novel of the twentieth century. In 1962, the novel was adapted for the screen and became a box-office hit. As a result, the screenwriter who adapted the novel for the screen, Horton Foote, won an Oscar for best screenplay. Other Oscars went to Gregory Peck for best actor and Henry Bumstead and Alexander Golitzen for best art direction. (E)

## Chapter 17
# The Alternatives

It shouldn't come as news to anyone that there are other types of film productions. You do not have to be stuck in the major-motion-picture mold if you don't want to be. On the contrary, becoming involved in alternative kinds of productions can be a marvelous way of gaining experience, and some of you might find it very rewarding in and of itself.

## The Independent Studio

Making a top-grossing film is not the only target to aim for, nor is working with the major studios, of which there are currently only seven. And the way the movie-making business changes, that number may not be accurate by the time this book is on the stacks.

Independent films, or indies, are different from the big-league movies. Independent studios may not be union signatories; their budgets are generally lower, and their financing comes from a variety of sources. (In the case of the major film studios, the money comes from the bank.) For a variety of reasons it is believed that the newer screenwriter is more apt to sell to an indie studio than to a major one.

**FACT**

There are many movies with a Hollywood or show business setting: *All That Jazz, The Bandwagon, Broadway Danny Rose, The Producers, The Entertainer, Funny Girl, The Bad and the Beautiful,* and *Two Weeks in Another Town.*

The spectrum of indie productions goes all the way from those who have strong distribution connections with the majors to those who have to beg, borrow, and scavenge for money to rent equipment and buy film stock. The philosophy of the indie production unit can be just as diverse and often the audiences are very seriously motivated moviegoers. Indie productions cover a wide variety of minority-based productions: gay, lesbian, and a vast ethnic and political diversity.

## Independent Producers

Independent producers have become a major force in the movie-production industry. The typical image of an indie producer is of a person strapped for cash who has to charge the last of his or her quickly diminishing production budget on a credit card. However, as many have become more successful, they enter bigger stakes, working for what are known as the mini-major studios; often, the major studios distribute their products domestically. These movies tend to leave the PG-13 mold of the basic audience-pleasing kind of movie, and so they are known to be more artistic than commercial.

# Artistic Visionaries

Indie producers and directors frequently are without the concern for profit that the major studios seek. Their credo tends to be the preservation of artistic integrity. Here are some of the better-known indie-minded filmmakers: Orson Welles, Sam Fuller, John Cassavetes, Ed Wood, and Radley Metzger.

The indie productions don't go unnoticed by Hollywood; Robert Redford's Sundance Festival in Utah has grown to be a virtual force as a showcase for independent producers. It draws players from the majors and includes films from around the world. While there are other indie festivals, it's probably fair to say that Sundance has upped the energy of the independent filmmaker.

## The Sundance Institute

The Institute supports the development and emergence of screenwriters and directors. Redford has said that over the past fifteen years there has been a noticeable change in the quality and sophistication of scriptwriting. Redford also said that in the Sundance Screenwriters Lab the focus is on the development of screenwriting because of the current poor scripts.

**ALERT!** If writers get involved with underfinanced independent producers, they should seek legal advice, particularly if they don't have an agent. A producer may ask for a free option. This means the producer has a fixed time, six months to a year, to shop the project around in an effort to raise finance.

An attitude not prevalent in Hollywood that comes from Redford is his respect for screenwriters. He had the writers of *Quiz Show* and

*A River Runs Through It* involved, even though they were not required to do rewrites. Redford is on record as saying that he doesn't believe writers should feel like distant cousins to a project when they turn their scripts in.

## The Stigma of an Art Label

The commercial/art argument has been with us for decades, of course. Another way to describe it is to say that what is popular is commercial and what is not is artistic, the implication being that people of lesser intellectual ability like what's popular.

As far as motion pictures are concerned, the same set of values apply, even within the industry, where it might be read in the trade press that a certain new film was an art house release. To the money people in Hollywood, getting the label "art" on a picture is a financial death prediction, although sometimes they are pleasantly surprised.

The adage "If you want to write, read" is equally as true for film. Only it would be, "If you want to write, view." It's important to watch films, new and old, good and bad. Be objective and at the end of the film, ask yourself: Why was that good, or why was that bad?

When so much money is at risk (most people could live a very comfortable life on the production budget of the average film), it's not surprising that the financial czars of the studios take a hard line when it comes to the subject matter of a proposed film. This has led to a sort of jumping on the bandwagon kind of mentality. In other words, if "boy" films are hot and suddenly making lots of money, then a studio chief might decree the green light to anything similar and hope it does as well. This follow-my-leader way of doing things, which is frequently the butt of cynical criticism from commentators who have never made a motion picture, is the direct result of trying to minimize something called "investment risk management."

Today, Hollywood remains disinclined to take risks because of rising production costs, which everyone complains about but nobody seems to do anything about. The trends established in the late 1980s continue with sequels and blockbusters. Thus there is room for the independents, who with their lower production costs, can and do take risks.

## It Can Work

A few years ago a group of completely unknown independent filmmakers got together to make a film; they managed to raise a budget of around $60,000. The picture did not have any of the polish of a major studio production, but then, it didn't cost quite the same to make. However, mainly through word of mouth, it built an audience. The box-office receipts have been said to total in the region of $140 million; the film was called *The Blair Witch Project*.

**QUESTION?**

**Is there any way to identify an independent film?**
If the plot is character-based, if there are limited special effects, no deafening romantic soundtrack, and if the actors look as if they are wearing their own clothes, it's pretty safe to bet the film you are watching is an indie.

Because of the economics of film production, European companies have being mounting coproductions. It is estimated that 150 films were made in France in the early 2000s using this type of financing. As the exhibition markets expand into new avenues, the need for a greater number of films (product) is rising. This, of course, means the need for a greater number of good scripts should follow.

Neophyte screenwriters should look beyond the traditional means of film production. While it may not be the safest way to go, provided a writer has good advice, there is every reason to presume that the outcome can be successful. Writers should not overlook the market if for no other reason than that the working environment is going to be far different from that of the majors.

# The Short Film

Some people initially look at the short film in the same way that others look at the short story. Because one is shorter than a feature film and the other shorter than a novel, they must both be easier to produce and write. Not quite. The difference between them is not just a question of length. In modern film it is the subject matter and market that tends to dictate the length of the film; in a short story the restriction is generally on the time and place of the action, as well as the number of characters and the depth of character development.

**FACT**

The Ultra-Low-Budget movie began to gain acceptance in the early 1990s when three features achieved successes at film festivals. This led to their producers finding theatrical distributors. The films were Nick Gomez's *Laws of Gravity*, Gregg Araki's *The Living End,* and Robert Rodriguez's *El Mariachi*. The budgets for these pictures ranged from $7,225 to $38,000.

## Types of Short Films

The Academy of Motion Picture Arts and Sciences, the outfit that gives out the Oscars, has a set of rules governing the definitions of acceptable product. Rule 19 covers special rules for the short film awards. The definition and categories are as follows:

1. A short film is defined as a motion picture that is not more than forty minutes in running time (including all credits).
2. An award shall be given for the best achievement in each of two categories:

**Animated Films.** An animated film usually falls into one of the two general fields of animation: character or abstract. Some of the techniques of animating films include cel animation, computer animation, stop-motion, clay animation, puppets, pixilation, cutouts, pins, camera multiple pass imagery, kaleidoscopic effects, and drawing on the film frame itself.

**Live Action Films.** A live action film utilizes primarily live action techniques as the basic medium of entertainment.

The definition goes on to say that documentary shorts will not be accepted in either category. It also states that previews and advertising films shall be excluded.

An annual film festival called WorldFest in Houston, Texas, claims to have given first honors to Spielberg, Lucas, Oliver Stone, David Lynch, and others. They promote a Short Film Showcase with a special review of a hundred new short and student films. The WorldFest people say that no other festival has such a discovery track record.

## The Documentary

At first glance it might seem odd that documentary films would need a screenwriter. Most people probably think that some bearded person, with a movie camera clutched in his hands, turns the lens toward a homeless person in the gutter and films away. It's not quite like that; if it were, it might be said that the person who turned his video camera on Rodney King was a documentary filmmaker.

The old saying about the computer, "garbage in, garbage out," applies equally to the documentary film. The very title, documentary, would indicate that it is a visual record of a factual set of occurrences. However, just like written reporting, much has to do with the degree of selection and/or omission.

The definition set by the Academy of Motion Picture Arts and Sciences reads:

1. A documentary film is defined as a nonfiction motion picture dealing creatively with cultural, artistic, historical, social, economic, or other subjects. It may be photographed in actual occurrence, or may

employ partial re-enactment, stock footage, still, animation, stop-motion, or other techniques, as long as the emphasis is on factual content and not on fiction.

2. A film considered to be primarily a promotional film, a purely technical instructional film, or an essentially unfiltered record of a performance will not be considered eligible as a documentary.

The two categories into which the documentary awards are divided are:

1. Documentary Feature: films more than forty minutes running time
2. Documentary Short Subject: films forty minutes or fewer (including all credits) in running time

## The Market

The eventual market for the completed production will depend to a certain extent on its financial backing. Is it a commercially sponsored film? Did the producer get the green light by a PBS station? Is there a distributor involved? Will the picture be entered into the various film festivals around the country?

Unless the writer is part of the production segment of the film, obviously his or her involvement is going to be minimal and limited to the purpose of the production. A great many documentary productions are made out of an intense emotional angst about the subject; for instance, the homeless and the starving. On the other hand, many are made by film school graduates anxious to put their education to work.

## The Motive

The attitude and motivation of the reporter/film person can very often, if he or she is not scrupulously alert, be subverted because of a serious need to prove a predetermined point. Thus, only that which supports the argument is given value, what doesn't is left out—omitted. It is because of this penchant in us all that drug researchers developed the double-blind system where neither the subject nor the dispenser knows who is getting what—the placebo or the real thing.

While sometimes something just happens without planning, that is not how you should go about writing and making a documentary. By all means take advantage of unplanned events, but don't count on them happening just when you'd like them to. If it is at all possible, do as much research as is practical.

As the writer of the production you should have a working knowledge of what equipment is going to be used on the shoot. Get to know the crew; it's probably going to be a compact one, which makes it all the more important that you work well together.

**FACT**

There is a trap waiting for any writer or filmmaker: It may be true, but is it real, or it may be real, but is it true? Another way of putting this is the question: Does the camera lie? The camera can certainly lie if that's what the operator wants it to do. As Wallace Stegner said: "There's as much biography in fiction, as there is fiction in biography."

## Preparing the Script

A lot will depend on how it came about that you are working on the script. Is the producer/director a friend? Were you hired because you're something of an expert in the subject of the film? Did you pitch the idea to the producer? Is your father putting up the money? Whatever the reason, it is essential that you involve yourself absolutely in the subject matter and purpose of the project.

If it is at all possible, it would be an excellent idea for you to work or be associated with the subject of the film. Obviously, this isn't always going to be possible. But say, for instance, the film is intended to be a documentary on the differences between New York City and London cabs. Naturally, you can do all the background research from the available records.

Then you should try to be taken on as a driver or, at least, a backup person in the office of the cab company in both cities, and that should include whatever vehicle service facilities they have. Get to know the cabbies, get to know the complaints, get to know the customers. By the time your research is finished you should be a good candidate for a permanent job. (It might come in useful while you're waiting for your next script assignment.)

> The long-term ambition of the scriptwriter should be firmly established in his or her mind. If the writer has decided to concentrate on writing documentaries, it will be a natural progression to look at becoming a director. Apart from taking on the responsibility, the attraction is having overall control and final cut.

## Script Format

What will be required from the scriptwriter will depend on the type of documentary production. If it is set up to cover an event, say the track test for a new racing car, then the structure will tend to be predetermined. The writer will initially probably be limited to preparing a shot list, establishing shots, preparation of the vehicle shots, and so on. He or she will then get involved in viewing the shooting, rushes, and the rough-cut edits.

Then it will be back to the keyboard to produce a narration script. By that time the writer should have a very good idea of what needs to be the accompanying audio to run over the visual shots. For example, the shot may be of the driver about to do some difficult technical maneuver. The narration might prime the audience on what the driver is going to try to accomplish.

## The IDA

The International Documentary Association is a nonprofit organization that has been around since 1982. Its purpose is to support nonfiction and video makers. If you intend to become a documentary film or video maker, it's just about essential that you get involved with the IDA. It has a tremendous resource capability, including in-depth information about submitting grant proposals to a seemingly endless list of national and international festivals. And it also offers what is called the IDA fiscal sponsorship, which means IDA will act as an overseer of progress of your production and as a distributor of funds.

Of course, to get access to any of these programs you have to become a member. Information about membership is available by phone at ☎ (213) 534-3600 or by mail, at 1201 West 5th Street, Suite M320, Los Angeles, CA 90017-1461. Membership fee includes subscription to the *International Documentary Magazine* (ten issues per year), and full-time student membership discounts are available as well.

The membership of the association includes people from across the production spectrum: producers, directors, writers, editors, technicians, and members of the public. To get more information, go to their Web site at ✑ *www.documentary.org.*

# Educational Films

The increased use of video often makes it difficult for the nonprofessional to distinguish between film and video, and in many ways it doesn't make a tremendous amount of difference to the scriptwriter. The technical debate on the comparable attributes of the two mediums takes on less importance in situations where the audience reception isn't crucial. This doesn't mean to say that second-best will do, only that the purpose of the production is not designed to reach the high technical standards of, say, *Saving Private Ryan.*

The power of film and video educational programs has proved their worth. A lecture that incorporates the study of a scientific instrument that would be impossible for students to see in an auditorium becomes simple when the instrument can be viewed either in the classroom or in the school audiovisual library, with a voice-over by the professor.

The kind of educational program that presents the greatest test of skill to the scriptwriter is one in which the information is delivered by an academic. The ditch that can easily be fallen into is the dreaded "talking heads"—two people, one delivering a message to the other, are photographed. One is showing how to do something, while the other person is photographed listening, and sometimes reacting, to what has been said. When edited together, the result is two talking heads talking and listening to each other.

"Talking heads" are the backbone of television talk shows and news broadcasts, where at least there is usually the option of cutting away to live action. The results are generally boring in direct relationship to the amount of live action included in the segment. A prescripted educational program has an advantage that the talk-show program generally lacks: time.

**FACT**

The essence of a successful educational program is in the mix between the on-screen visual and the off-screen audio narration, both integrated into the on-camera appearances of the personalities involved in the presentation of the material. Two people talking to each other on camera sitting against a backdrop is a recipe for failure.

## What We Mean

Here is an actual program example: A bank wants a series of programs that demonstrate to their lenders what a client looks for in a lender (the business of banks is lending money). By the time the professional scriptwriter has been hired the format has been decided upon: The bank expert will be on camera interviewing the client. Immediately, the scriptwriter sees the potential for a boring "talking heads" series of programs.

The scriptwriter proposes that each client be interviewed on the site of her or his business. The scriptwriter will script what will become a series of "cutaways" in which the client, on his or her own, will be involved. The shots will show the client at work; in one case a cattleman in Montana will be shown on horseback, out in the prairie, inspecting his cattle. The question-and-answer segments will then be laid over the visuals as voice-overs.

The result was interest from the audience because they became involved in the client's business. Not exactly complicated—in fact very simple—but the technique altered what could have been a very dry program into one that was quite the opposite. It can be seen from this example why television networks strive so hard to hire personalities their audiences find attractive; something or somebody has to balance out the "talking heads."

# Writing and Producing Your Own Film

The idea of making your own film can be intoxicating. It is presumed that you have spent all the time necessary to learn the practicalities of filmmaking. You know what the camera is capable of doing and you know how important editing will be to the final product. Perhaps you have practiced with a low-cost video camera, which has given you the feel for recorded images.

You should have immersed yourself in indie films and read all the literature you could get hold of. You have been on the Internet, joined indie chat groups, and subscribed to message boards. In other words, the obsession that filmmakers should have has immersed you. Now you feel ready to embark upon one of the most exciting projects in your life: You are to become an independent filmmaker.

At this point you have probably become fixated on the subject of your film. It is something you feel very deeply about; you want to make some kind of statement about it. This is essential because the enthusiasm that comes with these feelings will serve to buoy you over the rough spots ahead. Unless you are independently wealthy or have a sponsor waiting in the wings, your first step will have to be finding the money to make the film.

**ALERT!**

Many writers who get involved in production very early on start to wear two hats: writer and director. It stands to reason, therefore, that indie writers learning the art of direction should pay particular attention to the direction of amateur talent. Documentaries and educational films, for instance, tend to have more than their share of "real" people in their productions.

## Finding the Finance

Step number one is writing a proposal, which is really very close to a business plan. The purpose is to present to the potential backer what the film is going to be about. What you will be writing here is a selling document, so it should be couched in business terms. Try to keep any artistic flavor to the minimum; people or companies with money are often wary about the artistic.

Keep in mind the adage, "What's in it for me?" Why should they put up the money, and what will they get from it? Perhaps the prestige of backing something they consider socially worthwhile would suit their philosophy. Some organizations have a standard package that they require be completed. Be absolutely sure that you include the type of credit you propose the backers will have on the film.

The best proposals are short, easy to read, and to the point. Do not ramble on—make every word count. Say why your project is needed and how it will meet that need. Outline the direct and indirect benefits to the sponsors. Cover the production, the members of the crew, and their achievements. If appropriate, include résumés in the package.

**ESSENTIAL**

The one advantage of raising the money to make a documentary is that it is easier to explain a documentary than a theatrical picture. Nonfiction films can be qualified and quantified; theatrical pictures are subjective and thus more difficult to explain. They also involve personal preferences. For a start, what if one of your potential backers can't stand a certain actor?

## The Budget

An essential item will be the budget; the backers need to know how their money is going to be spent, which is not an unreasonable request. There are a number of factors, such as the following, you should have in place before the budget is even calculated.

- How big of a crew will you need?
- Will the production be union or nonunion? (Nonunion will produce a much lower budget.)
- Who owns the equipment you'll need? (If you are using your own, then you don't need to include rental costs.)

If the production is going to be a sizable one, then it would pay you to use the services of an experienced production manager. You will probably have to pay the fee for the manager out of your own funds to aid in the proposal. However, if the production is going to be complicated, it would be prudent to have a production manager onboard and therefore part of the budget.

## Accuracy

It should go without saying that it is essential that your budget be accurate; don't underestimate it with the idea that the less money requested, the more likely you'll be approved. That's a very shortsighted policy, which could easily result in worrying endlessly all during production that you are going over budget, and where does the shortfall come from?

In most cases your proposal, including the budget, will become part of the legal agreement between you and the backers. Included in the proposal should be estimates of the production time frame: How long will the film take to make? Again, don't fool yourself by giving a short time frame, which could lead to telephone calls and e-mails asking when the picture is going to be finished. The same problems that can beset a big theatrical production, over budget and over time, could strike your production, too.

**ALERT!**

Although the money involved if you are mounting a self-production might be less, you should still do a budget. Don't let the idea of making a film, and all the excitement that it will generate, blind you to the practical fact that there will be bills to pay, however small you think they will be.

## A Treatment

In just the same way as you would write a treatment for a theatrical film pitch, so you need one for an independent picture, irrespective of subject matter. The treatment must be part of your proposal. Keep in mind that it will not only outline what your production is about and is going to accomplish, but will be a blueprint against which your budget will be referred.

For example, if you intend traveling with your production crew 100 miles upstate, your treatment will cover the necessity for filming an aged, disabled character you need to interview. The budget for that film about cabs in New York City and London would obviously have to include travel expenses. The treatment would cover the reason and purpose for the location travel.

## Chapter 18

# Writing for Television

**S**ome people presume that writing for movies and television is pretty much the same, but it's not quite that simple. Some writers are much better at writing for television, while others succeed writing for film. To find out which one you are best suited for will take perseverance. This chapter will explore the area of writing for television.

# A Historical Outline

In 1927 the first television program was transmitted by wire from Washington, D.C., to New York City. Four years later, NBC got into the business and by 1939, it became the first broadcaster to use telephone lines to relay television signals. From that point on, television was off and running.

The 1950s were a pivotal period for the television industry as CBS and ABC joined NBC in competing for viewers. The number of viewers set the advertising rates—the more viewers, the greater the fee charged for advertising time, a concept that hasn't changed (with the exception of paid cable channels and public television stations). But back then, a single company could sponsor an entire program, so you had shows like *The Colgate Comedy Hour* with Donald O'Connor and the *U.S. Steel Hour*.

The Public Broadcasting Service (PBS) was founded in 1969. It is governed by a board of directors made up of broadcasting professionals as well as other citizens. PBS is a private, nonprofit American corporation whose members are the public television stations of the United States and other allied territories. PBS itself does not produce programming; that's done by its member stations.

## The Golden Age of Television

At first a novelty, television soon became the current wonder. Audiences would crowd around television sets at specified times in the evenings to watch comic artists such as Milton Berle and Ernie Kovacs. During the same period, color was introduced. Just as importantly, the creative aspects of television underwent a revolution. The period, the 1950s and 1960s, has become known as the Golden Age of Television.

Programs like *The Ed Sullivan Show, This Is Your Life, Lassie, Sgt. Bilko* with Phil Silvers, and *Playhouse 90*, culminating toward the end of the 1950s with Rod Serling's *The Twilight Zone,* caught the imagination of audiences all over the country. Television suddenly became a major threat to the movie business. There was no need to go out for entertainment—it was right there, in your own living room.

Many famous film actors got their start in television. In 1949 a twenty-four-year-old Marlon Brando starred in *I'm No Hero*, which was produced by the Actors' Studio. Other actors who got their start in television were Paul Newman, Susan Strasberg, and Steve McQueen.

A contributing factor to the freedom and standards of television arose from the economics of production. Television programs were relatively inexpensive to produce: A half-hour series might only be a quarter of the cost of a film. Then, too, there were the physical limitations of the television screen, which was not geared to lavish, expansive scenes and vistas. As often happens, restrictions gave creativity a chance, and television was becoming more and more popular, drawing in viewers who would tune in each week to see what would happen to the characters of their favorite show.

## The Cable Channels

The advent of HBO with its uncut, advertisement-free movies changed the way the studios and producers constructed their financial projections; television had become a source of revenue. Independent producers suddenly had another pool of income to dip into and the data showed that independent movies drew large audiences, particularly in the eighteen- to thirty-four-year-old age groups advertisers wanted to reach; the market was expanding all around.

It wasn't long until the television industry was contracting with Hollywood to make movies exclusively for them. The made-for-television films cost the networks far less to finance than it cost them to rent Hollywood blockbusters. Television could offer a much larger audience at one screening than Hollywood could ever match. Even actors had to consider the visibility television offered over the established movie release.

The expansion in the number of channels available on cable will, in the long run, increase the amount of product needed to feed their audiences. This, in turn, increases the market potential for writers. Today's writers have to be continually aware of the expanding possibilities for their talents and services. Many of the cable channels are and will be genre oriented; as it stands, the outlook for writers appears, for a change, as if it will expand.

# Television Writers

Unlike the motion-picture industry, in the early days of television the writer was recognized as a talent and respected as such. The creative centers and production hubs were then based in New York and the writers came from the local areas. Often they were playwrights and radio dramatists. The written word was a major force in the early creative drive of television.

But as the television networks and their affiliate stations expanded throughout the country and gained popularity and financial success, a rift occurred between the creative and the business side.

**E ALERT!**

Television has become an integral part of our lives. It not only reports on the news, it tends to shape it. Political candidates couldn't exist without it. Its effect is immediate and repetitive. Movies have made their peace with it because it has given them the means to improve their bottom line. In short, they need each other.

As the potential for profitability grew, so did the ownership of television companies and its allied forces. The conglomerate fever spread to the point where a company—AOL Time Warner being a prime example—might own an immense worldwide collection of entertainment companies.

## Why Writing for Television Is Attractive

In a nutshell, the advantages held out by writing for television are simple—money and more of it. If that happens to be your main ambition in life as a writer, then in many ways writing for television will simplify your approach to achieving it. There are writers who want to make a difference, to comment in depth on the human condition; that might mean running into some difficulties.

The fee for a single network half-hour prime-time drama pilot script can range from the Writers Guild scale minimum of $28,687.50 to $250,000 for established writers. While that may sound absolutely wonderful, and it is, it may be the only income you receive for a few years of going through endless rejections. As each year goes by without another sale, the amortized annual income gets more and more stretched, until you might have been better off learning plumbing as a trade.

**FACT**

According to Laubach Literary Action, the average kindergarten student has seen more than 5,000 hours of television, having spent more time in front of the TV than it takes to earn a bachelor's degree. According to the U.S. Department of Education, 44 percent of all American adults do not read one book in the course of a year.

If you did something similar in the film industry as a drama pilot script for television, and were paid the WGA Theatrical and Television Basic Agreement rates, this is what you might receive: Original Screenplay, Including Treatment: $48,731 to $91,408. Of course, all sorts of conditions and events can bump those figures out of the ballpark. Nevertheless, it can be seen why many writers are now gravitating to television in its various forms.

## The Wonder of It All

There's another great benefit to writing for television. One of the most wonderful aspects about it is the feeling you get from knowing how many people have sat in their living rooms watching what you wrote. Not only that, but you have the knowledge of how many professionals in television have approved of what you have written as it passed along the line and was green-lighted for production. Then there are all those actors who have spoken your words with such conviction and emotion.

## Educate Yourself about Television

Never overlook the prep work you should be doing. It's amazing the number of producers who have reported how many of the spec scripts sent in look as if the writer had only read the *TV Guide* description.

Try a different analysis tack, this one based on the dramatic content of a program. Pick a top running television show that's in reruns so that a segment is on every day. *Murder She Wrote* would be a good one because its dramatic structure is so consistent. You will note that the major characters are always the same. They all talk in the same way, dress the same, and have the same habits.

Episodic dramas usually run to sixty minutes and have four acts plus a teaser and tag. If the program is up for syndication possibilities, there may be five acts to accommodate more advertising breaks. The average script length is around forty-eight to fifty-four pages.

## Structure for Television Writing

Most television writing is done for shows and series that have a set cast of characters, so instead of developing entirely new stories, you have to come up with new ideas for the same basic concept. When it comes to writing for sitcoms and/or a series, a new writer doesn't fix what isn't broken, unless it happens that a major character leaves the show for some reason and a replacement has to be created.

The television writer has to structure the story around commercial breaks, which means that for sitcoms there may be a two-act structure and for a television movie, one of a series, perhaps a seven-act structure. The budding television scriptwriter is urged to watch and analyze a variety of programs, from sitcoms to high drama. Pay particular attention to the structure of each because that is what you will be expected to write to.

Come up with an answer for each type of program you are researching, and pay attention to the following factors:

- Length (in minutes)
- Number of commercial breaks
- How long each commercial break lasts

## Breakdown of Acts

The number of commercial breaks will give you the ballpark for number of acts. Of course, the length of the breaks for commercials can be expanded or retracted, depending on the station and time of exhibition. An episodic comedy is about thirty minutes long and consists of two acts. It has a teaser and a tag. Generally the length is twenty-six pages if on film, forty-two if shot on tape.

**FACT**

There are three categories of comedy: low comedy, which is full of coarse jokes, boisterousness, and buffoonery; high comedy, which is witty, subtle, and polished; and comedy of manners (see Noel Coward and Oscar Wilde). Stand-up comedy is a form of delivering comedy. Sitcoms are generally in the low-comedy category.

The number of acts in a structure is relative to the kind of program. It is also relative to whether the program is initially for the networks or cable—commercials or not. Obviously, you would know in advance what kind of program you are aiming to do. Or, if you're lucky, you've been hired to write and know in advance.

## The TV Script

Scripts for television vary in layout; part of this is because some programs are taped, others are shot on film. If you are inclined to have a go at the episodic or situation comedy segments of the television arena, you should understand that the executives will be looking for network-approved writers; they go with what they know. This is particularly so if the show is a new one; they have enough to worry about without testing the waters with fresh writing talent. But once the show has become established, the situation changes.

For established shows and series, the script layout is very close to the one used in a spec script for movies. At the beginning of your script, just as in a film script, start by typing FADE IN. It's usually the form to follow that with the teaser (see following section) and then break to a new page, which is titled ACT ONE (at center top). Some production outfits like their writers to type END OF ACT ONE about three spaces after the actual end of the act. You would then go to a new page and repeat the opening with ACT TWO, and so on.

It would be prudent, particularly if you have an agent who can do this for you, to get hold of a copy of an old script from the series you are trying to write for. That way you won't have to guess what the producers prefer. You will also have to know how many acts the show you are writing for is structured for.

It can't be emphasized enough how important it is to keep studying the television programs you would like to work on. Start taping them, particularly the comedy ones. You then have the opportunity of fast-forwarding to check on the timing of the gags or situations.

## Tag and Teaser

This is a simple television vernacular to be learned. The first term is the *teaser.* This is a short opening segment (about a minute or so) that introduces the characters and implies the action that's coming up. Remember, this is television and a viewer can very easily switch channels. Make the teaser count, so that the viewer is interested enough to stick around, or at least keep flipping back.

Once you've reached the end of your episode script, you have to create the opposite of a teaser, called a *tag.* A tag usually runs for a few minutes; its function is to wrap up the show and its resolution. Sometimes the tag is set up on a humorous, upbeat note. Sometimes there might be a voice-over doing a promo as in, "And now scenes from next week's episode."

It should be obvious how important it is to research the show or program you might be writing for, or even one you'd like to pitch for, before you put your fingers to the keyboard. If you are not experienced in judging the passage of time relative to the scene or segment you are writing, get yourself a stopwatch and start timing and making notes on the teasers and tags on other programs.

# Movie of the Week

A television network has the option of purchasing a blockbuster film from a studio, usually for an extortionate amount of money. Because the networks are under restrictions that dictate what is permissible to say and show on the air, these films then have to be edited for television. However, the networks have another option—they can commission their own made-for-television films. These movies are often known as Movies of the Week (MOWs).

Movies of the Week are 120 minutes long. They consist of six to eight acts of equal length. The usual length is from 101 to 110 pages, film format. The number of MOWs has increased tremendously at both broadcast and cable networks. An MOW can even act as a pilot to evaluate if a series developed from it might fly, which, of course, reduces the overhead of just making a new pilot series.

In the short run, it costs the networks less to produce their own films to suit the conditions under which they can show them than it does buying from the studios. In addition to that, a brought-in blockbuster has to be edited into the six- to eight-act structure to accommodate the networks' advertisements, thus adding to its initial cost. When the drawbacks are added up, the bottom line comes out, for once, on the side of the writer: more MOWs, more work.

# Pitching Your Work

Before you can try to be hired as a freelance scriptwriter or try to land a job as a writer on a series, you have to produce something that can be evaluated. Nobody is going to hire you just because you have all the enthusiasm in the world and figure how nice it would be to write for television. Not, that is, unless you happen to be the personal friend of a major stockholder in the company.

Keep in mind that nowadays the networks are permitted to produce their own TV series. They used to be prohibited from doing this. The fact that broadcast networks are now producers, of course, changes the playing field for writers. Cable and satellite networks are producing their own series as well, all of which should mean more potential work for writers.

## Breaking In

It is almost obligatory to have an agent in order to break in to the episodic or situation comedy market. But whichever you want to make a pitch for, it is essential that you produce sample scripts. These are not to be treated as spec scripts you want to sell, but as samples of your work that demonstrate your talent and ability to produce. Now, it's important that you use some common sense here.

How would you look at a sample script if you were an executive on a successful show? Naturally, you would have a critical stance and would compare the submitted script to your show. So it's not a good idea to write a sample script for the existing show that you'd like to write for. There are enough roadblocks without creating any of your own. The answer is to have a script that's similar in theme to the ones on the show you'd like to work on, but not versions of the same.

## The Formula

Before you start writing the script you are going to use as a sample of your work, try to get hold of the show's bible. It will tell you the limitations of the characters, what they can do and cannot do. It will describe the structure of the program and even give advice about the number of pages that should go to make each act. Some might even tell you that every fifteen pages in a seven-act structure, something exciting should happen, or some big conflict should occur—like a cliffhanger, to be resolved after the commercial break (to persuade the viewer not to switch channels, at least until they have the answers).

You will find out that this is not applicable if the program you are writing samples for is a cable show, as there is no need to make accommodation for advertising. Neither will you find restrictions of certain kinds of dialogue and action that are frowned upon. Some successful television scriptwriters, many of whom used to write exclusively for the movies, prefer to leave the networks alone because they feel the restrictions get in the way of their artistic ideals.

You will note that just as the plot point system in a three-act movie structure is the form, so the same philosophy exists in the seven-act structure of this type of programming for television. The similarities don't stop there. Once you have completed your sample scripts you are ready to pitch them, which is virtually identical to the way you would operate if you were pitching a spec film script to a movie producer in Hollywood.

## The Production Cycle

As the networks tend to work to a production schedule, it makes sense to work around the way most of them produce. The development cycle is generally from fall to midwinter. This is when pilot scripts for new series are commissioned and developed. If you don't have an agent, then scour the trade papers, which run news on what's on the upcoming slate.

**QUESTION?**

**What if I don't have an agent?**
The next best thing is to have friends in the business—anyone with a sharp ear will do. Bug them, if you have to, to find out what's in the works.

From January to April a few selected scripts are chosen for production as pilot episodes. This is a terrible time for the new scriptwriter if she has a script in contention, because she has to hang around wondering if her pilot is going to make the list for a production order. That doesn't mean you are suddenly in the business. Very few pilots make it to series status.

Most of what goes on in this period, and all through May, is beyond the scriptwriter's control. There will be people to whom the producers owe a big favor, there will be stars who want or need work—in fact, any one of a whole list of people who have degrees of leverage will have far more influence than you on what pilot goes forward or not.

By September, some of the pilots make the broadcast schedule, but even these shows aren't considered home and dry. More and more, pilots are given only short production orders and if they don't make it with the audiences, say within four episodes, they are pulled in a hurry. Such is the competition, which has become fierce. By wintertime, wobbly series are being replaced by shows held in reserve for just such an occasion.

## The Practical Stuff

Let's say that, wonder of wonders, the program executive liked your samples and is going to give you the opportunity of writing perhaps two scripts for the show. Now is the time for even more research; try to get hold of back episodes of the program. If it's a new show, that shouldn't be too difficult. Someone at the network or cable station can fix that for you. This is almost going to be like filling in a census form, and the answers are going to be just as important. What's the audience demographic (this should include the social strata)? What's the feel and style of the show? Is it lighthearted, serious, or does it deal with social issues?

How is the hour-long program filled out? Is there one solid plot line or subplots? Study the major characters until you know them like your relatives. Are there back stories to the characters? If so, do they have relevance to their lives now? Make a list of all the plot lines from previous episodes, just to be sure you don't repeat them.

## Write What You Know

While you should have in mind the type of program you are going to write, so that the number of acts can be predicted, put that aside for a minute. When you are starting out it will probably be advantageous for you to write your spec work in the subject matter that is close to you and in which you feel most comfortable. Maybe you are really well informed about crime stories, or medicine, or human nature stories—people in trouble and how they get out of it. Whichever, just keep it close to home.

Your feeling about the story will be reflected in your confidence, which, in turn, will be shown in your writing. A reader can tell if the writer is uncertain; it'll show. You are less likely to exhibit this lack of confidence if you stick to what you know. Later, when you are an ace, you can move on to any subject you like.

**FACT**

Some of the lowest-ranking shows on television bring in audiences of six million or so viewers. Converted into dollars at the movie box office, those figures would eclipse most middle-of-the-road movies, and that is calculated on just one night's exposure on television. It's no wonder that the climate in the offices of the networks is frenetic.

## Writing for Young Audiences

The networks all aggressively seek out the same demographic audience, the eighteen- to thirty-four-year-old age group. In doing that, they have been copying the cable networks. This means producing what are called narrow-casting programs, which target that audience age group. These are the people advertisers love, and the programs that produce them are the ones in demand.

Scriptwriters are urged by their agents to come up with concepts that suit those criteria. At the same time, observers criticize the system that has media buyers who are under thirty-four constantly seeking the programs that fit only that demographic. A typical successful hit program that does fit the mold would be *Ally McBeal,* whose protagonist is in her twenties.

It stands to reason that as a general rule, like seeks like, so it should come as no surprise that the people who green-light pitches are, just as in the movies, in the same demographic as the intended audience. A gray-haired writer without a superb track record of success sitting across from someone who could be a son or daughter might not do too well.

## Chapter 19

# Welcome to Hollywood

The first thing that has to be understood is that the movie business is that: a business. And the sole interest of this business is to make money by getting people to come to the movies in gigantic numbers. How does this apply to you? Well, it's important to know that Hollywood needs you to come up with film scripts that can make those kinds of movies—box-office hits. And you need to be able to sell your work to the industry.

## The Studio

Hollywood has been called a state of mind rather than a place, and there's a strong element of truth to that. It should be established that Hollywood is a generic term that refers to a sort of center where movies are made. However, American movies are actually made all over the place: San Francisco, New York, Toronto, London, Paris, Rome, and elsewhere throughout the world. But wherever they are made, the mentality is the same. And as you already know, wherever the film production is taking place, it can't happen without those 120 three-hole-punched pages—the script.

**FACT**

When the word "Hollywood" is used in the business, it typically represents the American motion-picture business. In many ways that's unfair, because there are many independents who are not "Hollywood-minded." Nevertheless, as far as screenwriting is concerned, there is little difference in spite of what may be thought.

Scriptwriters in the studios of yesterday came to work in the morning and were paid by the week. In every studio there was a writers' section or wing. If a writer deserved it, he or she was assigned a secretary to type up clean drafts of handwritten or very roughly typed pages. Studio heads always worried that their writers weren't doing enough work; and in some cases, they had a reason for worrying.

## Literature and the Movies

Some of the most famous literary names in America spent time in Hollywood, with varying degrees of success. These include Nunnally Johnson, Dudley Nichols, F. Scott Fitzgerald, William Faulkner, Nathanael West, and Aldous Huxley. As it turned out, not all the big-name literary writers could write screenplays. It's also fair to say that few of the established screenwriters had any success writing novels.

This would seem to confirm that literary talent is not a necessary ingredient for a scriptwriter to have. What is absolutely necessary is visual imagination together with the knowledge of how movies work and how a film is put together. There are many stories about literary luminaries arriving in Hollywood expecting to polish off a screenplay in a few days. In part, this attitude was the result of disdain the rest of society held for the filmmaking industry.

## The Majors

Hollywood emerged into the film scene relatively early; by the 1930s, it ruled the cinematic landscape, and yet it was made up of only a few big studios on the West Coast. These studios soon became known as the majors, and they included the following giants:

- Warner Bros.
- Columbia
- Metro-Goldwyn-Mayer (MGM)
- Paramount
- Twentieth Century Fox
- RKO
- Universal

Willam Wyler, who was one of the most successful directors ever, had a reputation for being a very sensitive director. His pictures, like *Roman Holiday,* had what was called "the Wyler touch." A screenwriter who was fed up with hearing about the Wyler touch is said to have gone to Wyler's office, thrown down 120 blank script pages, and said, "Now give those the Wyler touch."

Each studio had vast lots that housed their production stages, sound recording, music, cinematographers, technical departments, and crew—in short, everything that was required to make movies on site. They also owned the cinemas that screened the movies they produced.

## The Changes

In the 1940s things changed radically when the government began its campaign to enforce antitrust legislation in Hollywood. As a result, the studios could no longer hold their own theaters. As far as the majors were concerned, the landscape went from bad to worse, until by the

1960s the independent film companies, or indies, had become established and thus opened up the whole production system.

But despite the changes, most of the majors survived and are still around, although now some are owned by a variety of other companies. They have been joined by Disney, Sony Pictures Entertainment, and, lately, by DreamWorks SKG. The number of pictures produced each year varies according to the economic climate, but roughly the figure is around ten to fifteen a year per studio.

**QUESTION?**

**What else was different in the studio days?**
The actors and actresses were all under contract. Their lives were virtually controlled by the studios, even to the point of when they could get married. All the publicity was under the studios' control; the studios generated all the photographs and public relations handouts.

The studios are no longer the restrictive family units they used to be. Now they may rent out their own studio space, finance independent productions, produce movies for television, and get involved in any other film projects they regard as profitable ventures.

Much of the criticism leveled against the big studios today is based on the assertion that the people running the studios don't know much about films. Back in the good old days the men who ran the major studios were film men; even though they may have started in the glove business, they knew about pictures. The three Warner brothers, Samuel Goldwyn, Louis B. Mayer, and many others knew what they were doing and were intimately involved in the work of their studios. At Twentieth Century Fox, for instance, producer and film mogul Darryl Zanuck had the reputation of being a great story editor.

Today, it's claimed, there are only business people and accountants running the studios. Their only concern is to appease the demands of the stockholders. Of course, people today forget that even back in the good old days, the studios had to listen to their investors in New York City and other financial centers.

# The Players

In Hollywood it's a good thing to be a player, even though it may not last forever. The upper-echelon players often make life insecure for lower-level players. Naturally, the power of the player is relative to his or her ability to make decisions. While one decision a player might be able to make is the allocation of a new personalized parking space on the lot, the prized position is to be able to "green light" a script, which could lead to the chance that it might actually be produced into a film.

It doesn't take a genius to grasp that when a business is full of beautiful and sometimes talented people who earn immense sums of money, the players make the ground rules. A player doesn't have to be an executive in a studio or in an independent filmmaker's office on Sunset Boulevard. One of the top-flight kinds of player is a movie star; as we all know, sometimes they can even become president of the United States.

A limited number of stars who become players are often on what Hollywood refers to as the "A List." Being on the A List leads to many good things; exposure, party invitations, free catered meals, and so on. Star players have the clout to approve or reject scripts. Their approval can mean that the studio player can be confident enough to green light a script.

> Rent a copy of Robert Altman's *The Player* (1992). Apart from being a highly entertaining picture with about sixty cameo appearances by Hollywood stars, it has a sharp satirical edge to it (Altman's signature). *The Player* is pretty close to the way things really are in Hollywood and provides insight into the way the industry works.

# The Front Office

The front office is where most of the big studio decisions are made, except, that is, from wherever the most chic watering hole in Beverly Hills happens to be at the time you are in town. If you manage to make your way into a front office, it's best to be accompanied by an agent or a lawyer. When you are up against those smooth and very persuasive Hollywood executives, it makes very good sense to have professional advice by your side. What you are also going to be dealing with is personality, yours and the other guy's. You should understand that a lot of money can be made in the movie business, even if you don't have any talent. Sure, you can rely on your talent, but you also need the business smarts to make it through the negotiation process.

This is true of any business, of course, but remember that the movie business is even tenser because the stakes are higher. There are very few businesses where even a novice has the possibility, just on the nod of one person, to make upwards of $100,000 on the delivery of 120 typed pages that constitute a film script.

## Dealing with the Committee Syndrome

In almost every business there are committees. Committees do not have a good name and are frequently the butt of stale jokes. A film production is a committee in furious action. The trouble, of course, is that everyone has an opinion and seeks to express it all the time. Whether or not anyone listens and takes any notice is in direct relationship to the amount of clout wielded.

**FACT**

Everyone in movies does business on the telephone. In the past, the big executives had those old-fashioned phones in their cars. Today, though, everyone in Hollywood has a cellular phone.

In a film, the power may be shared by some of the following: the studio or independent producer, the director, the major stars, and all of the people in their personal lives. It follows that for a writer to be able to maneuver through the labyrinth of power takes a certain personality. Unfortunately, writers generally do not fit the profile of a power broker.

## Trying to Circumvent the System

If you happen to be the author of a spec script in production and you live in the middle of Ohio and do not have a heavy-hitting Hollywood agent, the best thing to be done is to hope they spell your name right on the credits and get on with the next spec script. However, if you are an ace schmoozer living on the outskirts, or even the in-skirts, of Malibu, things could be different. But if you are not only the author of the script but also of the novel on which it is based, do not think your clout rating has improved. If anything, it could have gone down a notch or two. Authors are considered by those in Hollywood to be intellectuals and therefore suspect. To handle the situation with any degree of success requires a change of perspective. Switch from trying to figure out how to deal with the committee yourself and instead figure out ways in which they should learn to deal with you.

The first attribute you should nurture within yourself is confidence. Never be demure, even if you are not sure you are correct; be incorrect with incorrigible confidence, except where money is concerned—there they will have you beat hands down. The main reason you will succeed will be because the opposition isn't well enough informed to contradict you.

## The Budget

As the studio signs up a film project, it is allotted a specific budget. The budget has many functions; one, obviously, is to slot expenditures into their appropriate categories. A major demarcation line that separates the expenditures is whether they are made before or during film production (when the film is being shot). The difference between these two types of expenditures is referred to as "above or below the line." (As it happens, film people are also referred to as being above or below the line.)

**ESSENTIAL**

Industry vernacular is a language all its own and includes terms like "dense," referring to scripts that are heavy in detail and hard to read. Another term, "good with story," is a tag given to those people who are bad at something else.

Expenses above the line are made prior to the shooting process, and one of these expenses is purchasing the screenplay—that's where you come in. Also included are the producers, director, stars, and other actors. If you want to generalize, "above the line" folks are all those who come before or immediately under the opening credits.

Below the line are the people who make the picture: the cinematographer, editor, assistant director, production assistant, and so on. They come after the opening credits, frequently running at the end of the picture, which nowadays is still doing its thing when audiences have fled the cinema. Caterers and car services are often on the list as well.

## Film Unions

The major studios are union signatories, which means they use only union talent and pay union wages; this adds about 30 percent to the budget. You don't need to be an accountant to work out how much this can add to the finished budget of a production. When the costs of promotion and distribution are factored in, it becomes very clear why a movie from plain paper all the way to silver screen can cost $40 million and change.

**ALERT!**

Research has shown that the best movie titles are made up of two or three words that include a name, whether it's of a person, place, or even animal. And in terms of genre, it appears that the most popular is drama.

The independent film companies may not be union signatories, which can help them to make do with lower budgets. The financing of indie pictures comes from a wide variety of sources: network and cable, foreign exhibitors and distributors, and private investors. Some productions still can't scrape together enough funds, and are finished courtesy of the director's credit card. Financing a film can be almost as creative as writing one.

# The Status of the Writer in Hollywood

The most difficult thing to accomplish is to create what is original. Anyone can adapt, change, or copy. In the film business they do it all the time, and even take credit for it. Writers in Hollywood work very hard on creating and polishing, putting the right words and stories together, yet many of them don't get the credit they deserve. Unfortunately, it must be said that the Hollywood industry doesn't hold screenwriters in great esteem.

Often, writers are taken for granted and their work is seen as something to work with, not a finished product. The opinion in Hollywood is that scriptwriters don't have much in the way of clout (the exception is if you are an Oscar winner), and so writers are pretty low on the prestige totem pole. Many of the people who can't write—agents, directors, actors, reviewers, and executives—will insist on putting their two cents in, invited or not. To repeat the adage: Every cabdriver in Los Angeles has a script in progress.

**FACT**

Somewhere in the region of 98 percent of all spec screenplays submitted to agents, readers, and/or directly to studios face rejection. Many are so bad, they would be rejected by your plumber. Reasons for rejection include handwritten manuscript, copious misspellings, eccentric grammar—and that's before we get to the script layout, let alone the story line.

## A Difficult Business

The status of the writer in Hollywood probably hasn't changed very much over the years. When Hollywood writers do gain prestige, it's usually when they decide to direct their own films. In fairness, the nature of the business where many people can have input to a picture doesn't help much. Another factor is the amount of money at stake.

For example, the reputation of a film executive rests on the success of a film he or she personally gave the green light to, and the project receives a budget of $10 million. The temptation to interfere must be immense—who could stand by and watch the process that will make or break your career?

**ALERT!**

Almost the only time a screenwriter's name gets into print is when there is an interview piece in a magazine devoted to the industry or to movie fans. In comparison, a book review is mostly about the author, not the publisher of the work. But that's the nature of film business—the screenwriter rarely gets a second thought.

Adding to the conflict of interest is the position of the director, who is responsible for the artistic as well as commercial success of the film. If the film's a failure, who knows if the director will ever get another project to work on. The pressures are there, and sometimes the players can't all agree on what's best. Unfortunately, the screenwriter is left out of these struggles. Once the studio purchases the script, it's pretty much out of the screenwriter's hands.

## The Director and the Screenwriter

If mutual respect exists between the writer and the director—and it often does—then the production will benefit. A good working relationship is generally a result of working together. It may even happen if the writer is on his or her first script and the director is an old hand at the game. In this case, the director may act as the writer's mentor.

However, be aware that there have been endless tales about the horrendous rows and shouting matches between writers and directors. It seems to be in the nature of the craft that the creative egos of the two are designed to clash. The problems stem from the number of opinions that get involved in the production. For instance, a writer will do a rewrite of scene 235 for the shooting schedule. He hands it to the director the night before the shooting. The director takes it to his home in Beverly Hills and on the way there shows it to the driver of the studio limo. When he gets home he shows the scene to his wife.

After a couple of cocktails before dinner, the director puts in a call to the writer, who takes it on the cellular phone in his car on his way home to Tarzana in the Valley. The director tells the writer in short order that the scene will have to be redone, it's just not what he wants. What he neglects to mention to the writer is that he hasn't actually read the scene himself.

## Dealing with Envy

Another part of the problem is the unexpressed, sublimated envy of the writer in the industry. After all, the writer is the only one who originates new material. To acknowledge that the picture you are working on is not really yours, but has been written by someone else, is difficult to stomach for many people. As some screenwriters have suggested, perhaps the reason they aren't allowed on the set is that people don't want to be reminded that the film was the screenwriter's idea.

All writers should rejoice in the fact that they originate—that's the difficult part; copying is a cinch. Nevertheless, the price is often that rejection is going to come, and many times it is justified. The minute you create and put what you create out there to be judged, you are open to criticism and disagreement.

## Who Wrote It?

It has always been the nature of the writing game that readers will praise a book, be really enthusiastic about it, but not know the name of the author. This is much the same in the movie industry—and perhaps even more so. When you've got a book, the author's name is right there on the cover. But when you rent a video or buy a DVD, the screenwriter's name is hidden in the credits. Film fans often remember the name of the director, but they rarely know who wrote the screenplay.

In a sense, this is because the screenwriter writes for the industry. By the time the film is made, it has been worked on by so many people that the script itself has taken a back seat to the actual movie, complete with actors, scenes, and dialogue. That's why the only time a screenwriter gets visibility is on Oscar night, and then there are only two of them up at the podium.

## The Best-Known Scriptwriters

The two most visible screenwriters are probably William Goldman and Robert Towne. Goldman wrote *Butch Cassidy and the Sundance Kid* (1969), *The Stepford Wives* (1975), *Marathon Man* (1976), and *All the President's Men* (1976). These were the most successful among many other screenplays and books. He also contributed additional uncredited work to many films as a script doctor. One of the reasons for William Goldman's celebrity, apart from the films he's scripted, is a book he published in 1983 called *Adventures in the Screen Trade: A Personal View of Hollywood and Screenwriting*. It has become more or less required reading for budding screenwriters.

Towne wrote *Bonnie & Clyde* (1967), *Chinatown* (1974), and many other films, both credited and uncredited. It's interesting to note that in 1997 Robert Towne was presented with the Writers Guild of America's Screen Laurel Award, the WGA's highest award in recognition of his body of work. Some other recipients have been Ruth Prawer Jhabvala, Waldo Salt, Woody Allen, Neil Simon, and Billy Wilder. The more recent recipients include Betty Comden and Adolph Green (2001). And who can forget two of the films they wrote, *Singin' in the Rain* and *The Band Wagon,* even if the names of the scriptwriters can't be remembered?

**FACT**

If you have time, rent *Annie Hall.* It's said to be Woody Allen's best film. Allen stars in his own film, along with Diane Keaton, who won an Oscar for best actress. The screenplay was written by Woody Allen and Marshall Brickman. In 1977, *Annie Hall* beat *Star Wars* for the Best Picture Academy Award.

## Writers Guild of America

If you are serious about screenwriting, you may consider joining the Writers Guild of America. This organization has a lot to offer. It represents published writers in motion pictures, broadcasting, cable, and new media and provides an online mentoring service, script registration, lists of agents, industry news, and lots more.

The Writers Guild of America has two branches, one on each coast; these are known as the Writers Guild of America, East, Inc. and the Writers Guild of America, West, Inc. Both branches have a Web site:

- Writers Guild of America, East: *www.wgaeast.org*
- Writers Guild of America, West: *www.wga.org*

Anyone can register a script with the WGA, which can provide additional copyright protection for five years at the cost of just over $20.

**ALERT!**

It may not be wise to have the copyright year on your script, particularly if it has been shunted around for a long time. You may not want everyone in Hollywood to know how long your work has been out in the world.

If you are the sort of person who likes to belong to professional organizations, you can, after your second script sale, apply for membership to the WGA. However, the price of membership is somewhat hefty, and there are both pros and cons to belonging to a writers' union, so you should give the matter reasonable thought

## The MPAA Rating System

The Motion Picture Association of America (MPAA) administers a rating system of content for each film submitted to its board. The film producer makes the submission; although submission is voluntary, most producers do go along with the board's decision, because without a rating the chances of a good distribution deal are slight. If there is disagreement, the director or distributor can appeal a particular rating. The board reviews the film as appealed and makes its final decision.

It would be good for you to be aware of each rating, what it represents, and the audience that is affected by the rating. The following are the MPAA ratings.

**G: General Audiences—All Ages Admitted.** Although the "G" rating doesn't necessarily signal a children's film, it does indicate that there is nothing in the picture that, in the opinion of the MPAA rating board, would be offensive to virtually anyone in terms of language, nudity, sex, and violence.

**PG: Parental Guidance Suggested. Some Material May Not Be Suitable for Children.** The rating indicates that parents need to inquire about the film before they let their children attend. While there may be nothing offensive in the film, the content may simply not be appropriate for young children.

**PG-13: Parents Strongly Cautioned. Some Material May Be Inappropriate for Children Under 13.** A sterner warning for parents, alerting them to be very careful about letting their preteen children attend a viewing.

**R: Restricted. Under 17 Requires Accompanying Parent or Adult Guardian.** This indicates that some adult material is contained in the film and that parents are strongly urged to find out if they think it is suitable for their children to accompany them.

**NC-17: No One 17 and Under Admitted.** The rating doesn't mean the film is obscene or pornographic—these are legal terms, so the board does not use them. However, if a film does contain excessive violence, graphic sexual content, or drug abuse, the board may rate it NC-17, which takes away the parents' choice to allow or prohibit their children from watching the film. Few mainstream films merit this rating, perhaps because most cinemas choose not to screen these movies.

Producers generally know what rating they are aiming for even before film production begins, and it may benefit you to keep this information in mind too as you are working on and marketing your script.

In spite of the apparent preference of Hollywood for producing films for the younger segment of society, PG-13–rated films made up only 49 percent of all released films in 2001, as more and more movies are rated higher for sexual content.

## Chapter 20

# Marketing Your Work

As you probably know, marketing means selling and the way to do it. As a screenwriter, you have two properties that are unique and require marketing. First off, you need to market your work. But, and this is less obvious, you also need to market yourself and your image and skills. Because the industry has become far more competitive than it used to be, new techniques have to be adopted in order to succeed.

## Creating a Plan

It is said that before you sell your first screenplay you should have written at least three. It is not required that you write them while hanging around the pool in Marina del Rey. You could very easily have been in a coffee bar in Billings, Montana. However, part of the education of a scriptwriter is how the business works and part of that is understanding, and perhaps being privy to, the undercurrent of snobbery and gossip that swirls around the best restaurant tables in Beverly Hills.

It would be wonderful if you could just call a studio, ask for an appointment, and take your brand-new spec screenplay in for a quiet discussion over a cup of tea. You may have been able to do it decades ago, but those days are long gone. Today, you can't just show up and expect to be heard. What you need is a marketing plan to get attention for yourself and your product. And there are a number of items you have to understand before you attack the market.

**FACT**

Here is S. J.'s Perelman's take on Hollywood: "It was a hideous and untenable place when I dwelt there, populated with few exceptions by yahoos, and now that it has become the chief citadel of television, it's unspeakable. A dreary industrial town controlled by hoodlums of enormous wealth, the ethical sense of a pack of jackals, and taste so degraded that it befouled everything it touched."

## Word-of-Mouth Advertising

The most powerful advertising/sales tool is word of mouth. People trust their friends and what they tell them. Think about this example. Let's say a movie did really well and the studio decided to produce the sequel. Unfortunately, as it often happens, they couldn't get the same screenwriter and director, or maybe the sequel idea wasn't that great, but for one reason or another the end result was that the sequel turned out to be a bad film.

The first week the sequel was released at the movie theaters, many of the viewers who had seen the first film went to see the sequel, and so it did relatively well. But the following week, the attendance was way down. What happened? Word of mouth was to blame. The viewers who went the first week killed it.

Word of mouth works the other way, too. Once in a while there is an independently produced film that has no publicity budget and opens at a few art houses, and then catches on, until it gets distribution into the mainstream movie theaters. These late success stories are known as *sleepers;* sometimes it takes a while for word of mouth to spread from the water cooler to the rest of town.

You can use the concept of "word of mouth" in your marketing plan. Try to get your name out, so that people in the industry are talking about you and your work. With enough perseverance, you may generate enough interest for an interview with a studio executive and—who knows?—maybe even a contract deal.

## Location, Location, Location

Using the word-of-mouth technique is difficult if you're not out in southern California. But don't give up your day job and move to Hollywood unless you suddenly come into a sizable amount of money.

If you live away from the typical American filmmaking areas, Los Angeles and New York, seriously consider using the agent route. (See Chapter 21 for information about finding an agent.) Nevertheless, you still have to look at your personality. At the same time, take note of what your grandmother probably told you: "You can't make a silk purse out of a sow's ear." Be as honest as you can with yourself and don't try to be something you're not; be genuine.

**QUESTION?**

**What about the Canadian market?**
If you happen to live close to the Canadian border, it is a good idea to consider the Canadian film market. For budget reasons, a lot of Hollywood movies are produced in Canada.

## The Out-of-Towners

It is a very nice idea to believe that talent will show and that all you need for success is for a reader in a prestigious agency or major studio to pick up your script and be absolutely overwhelmed by it. The problem is that if he or she sees an out-of-town postmark, the odds are that your friendly reader will suddenly be very much underwhelmed. Actually, it's terrible, but in a way understandable. Hollywood is a community that thinks only movies or television. Writing for movies requires a good understanding of how the business works, and to get that it helps if you live in the environs.

You will not add to your industry education by studying *People Magazine,* although if you think it's important you might get up to par on who is seeing whom. What would help would be to take subscriptions to "the trades." These are industry trade publications: *The Hollywood Reporter* and *Daily Variety.* There are now two versions available: print and Internet. You can start off by just looking around their Internet sites to get a feel, but to access any valuable information you have to subscribe.

# The Power of Socializing

If you do happen to live relatively close to Hollywood or New York City, once you have completed your spec script the time has come to mix. You have to start talking, and anyone will do, from the nice man collecting the garbage (he may know people you would like to know), to your hairdresser, mail person, and even your dentist. Remember, many of those people have children who may go to school with the children of persons whom you would like to read your screenplay.

It is said that everyone in Hollywood has a screenplay in the works. But you'll also hear that people in the industry have only one topic of conversation. Along those lines, it would be a good idea to try and mix with below-the-line people. The two professions that have most insight into how pictures are made are cinematographers and editors. They know what will play and what will be cut.

You could learn as much about writing a screenplay from the technical types on a film as you could from almost anyone else. Technicians tend to socialize with their own kind, and they have the inside track on all the gossip, a good cocktail party plus. In many ways, mixing with below-the-line people could be a far more rewarding experience, both practical and on a friendship basis, than with above-the-line people. The only competition a scriptwriter has is another scriptwriter.

The phrase "He ended up on the cutting room floor" originated from editors. This is why editors can be a tremendously valuable resource of expertise for screenwriters. Editors can make or break a scene and the actor in it. Read about editors and what they have to say about their craft.

## Making Contacts

Contacts are the name of virtually every game. As the saying goes, "It's not what you know, it's who you know." That couldn't be more accurate than in the movie industry. The problem is, most people don't have the right kind of movie contacts. That means you have to establish some.

The first step will be research; how can you get contacts if you don't know who to seek out? Doing the research necessary to produce contacts is rather like being a detective. The best detectives get their results from good and persistent legwork. In doing this kind of research it is very important to keep copious and accurate records.

Here is a list of major sources to try for contacts:

- Agents
- Managers
- Producers
- Production companies with deals at the major studios
- Independent producers
- Independent production companies that finance their own work
- Directors

And that's just a start—there's no reason to stop here. To make contacts you have to keep at it and not give up.

## Socializing Via the Internet

Maybe you could somehow strike up a friendship with some honest person in the general Los Angeles area (a possible alternative might be New York, which is fast becoming the hub for television, with movies on the side). The idea, of course, is that you can use this person's address as a mail drop. As this could turn out to be a burden on the lovely person, you could try an alternative.

The Internet, as most people know, means having an Internet Service Provider and a screen name. Your Internet address is, up to a point, anonymous, and if you want to get really cagey you could check the L.A. weather so you could drop remarks in your e-mail about the temperature and such. Just be sure you don't slip up and complain about the snow in Montana. There are other drawbacks that you face if you pull this kind of trick: attachments. Not too many agents or studios are going to accept them, which poses a problem with sending screenplays.

**QUESTION?**

**What does it take to beat the Hollywood system?**
Lack of emotion. They have you before you move because you care. One ploy: Have caller I.D. on your phone so you don't have to answer it if you don't choose to when they call. Make them wait; that's something they don't understand from someone new to the game. And always keep your cool; never swear.

Again, the sensible way out of all this is to have an agent in the L.A. area who is not going to be thrown that you live several states away. He or she will be sensible enough not to bandy about that you are not a local, and by the time your first script is being bid on, it won't matter. Once that happens, it will suddenly become the chic thing to have a screenwriter from Montana on the credits. In the end, for all the ploys everyone may use it is going to be the weight of your story that will tip the scales in your favor.

# Cold Calling

Once you've done your research and your socializing, you'll have a few contact numbers. The next step is to call those people. Go over your script in your mind, so that you don't fluff on the phone, but be sure you aren't going to sound like a sales recording. Make notes on a pad to look at when you call someone, so you don't leave out any salient points you should be making. (Like what? Your log line, of course.) Set up some kind of record-keeping files on your computer, if you have one, to keep track of whom you call and what was discussed.

It's important not to trust your memory, so make notes about personal matters as well as business ones. For instance, if a reader at a studio told you not to bother calling back because she would be off on vacation, ask her where she is going and when she'll be back. Make a note of the relevant dates so that you can call back at an appropriate time to find out how the holiday went.

You should be sure your telephone voice is friendly. Try to build up a relationship with the people you call. Of course, try not to overdo it— be casual, cool, and calm. The more calls you make, the better you'll get at them, so it's best to start out with the less important contact numbers.

You need to have notes of the research telephone calls you have made and their the results. You will also want to know to whom you have sent query letters, when, and what response you got, if any. Also keep track of all the names and titles, and correct spellings.

## Make Every Call Count

Whoever you speak to and whatever the results, always, always ask for a referral. Some people you speak to will give you a referral just to get you off the phone. That doesn't mean it's useless. When you do speak to the person to whom you were referred, give the source; for example: "So and so at Disney (or wherever) gave me your name and said you might be interested. . . ." If you draw a blank with this call, don't hang up until you have asked them, too, for a referral.

Always remember that the one person in an office who has the best information is the secretary. A good secretary knows everything that goes on and just may be your best contact. Being an intelligent person, you will always treat people on the other end of a telephone with respect. Never brush off a secretary or receptionist, or act like you're some superstar; as far as you are concerned, the secretary is frequently the most important person in the company.

# Contact by Mail

Another way to contact the studios is to send them your work by mail. One rejection-reducing device is to be sure you send your work to someone who might be in the market for it and thus be sympathetic. For example, it would probably not be a good ploy to send your spec script on the voluntary destruction of all armaments to the head of the NRA (National Rifle Association) film department. It's useless to send an adult film that may get an NC-17 rating to Disney, so make sure you do your research and find out which studios and producers may be interested in your particular line of work.

## The Query Letter

There are many people who think query letters are a waste of time. Their reasoning is that if a query letter arrives on a producer's desk, the secretary is going to open it, take one look, and either throw it in the wastebasket or, if there is a SASE envelope enclosed, send back a template rejection letter. In many cases, that is exactly what happens—but sometimes a query letter can make a huge difference in the life of a screenwriter, so it may be advisable to take your chances.

It might be worthwhile to consider the psychology of the situation. Without scripts, movies would not be made and studios would not stay in business. People in the moviemaking business need ideas and scripts—as long as these are ideas and scripts that will make movies that sell. What they really want, of course, is to latch on to a better script than the competition.

All moviemakers are bombarded with outlines, synopses, endless log lines, and scripts, most of which come via agents. Word travels very quickly in the industry and pretty soon almost everyone knows what is doing the rounds. What they would all die for is the idealistic dream: An envelope is opened and out of it come a few typed pages. The recipient picks them up and starts to read what they figure is yet another piece of nonsense. *Just a minute,* they think, *this is good—this is very good. Who is this person?*

**QUESTION?**

**Do you have to write custom query letters?**
Each letter should be personally addressed to an individual, but the rest of the letter doesn't have to be personalized. The content would be the same, irrespective of who the recipient is and what they do. After all, it all boils down to "Do you want to read my spec script?"

The interesting thing about this little piece of daydreaming is that both sides have it: the writer and the producer. The more sophisticated they are the less they believe it will ever happen, but the idea of it never really fades. The reason is that it has actually happened, therefore the thinking is, it could happen again—and so it could, and why not with your script?

## The Pitch

You are now fully prepared to make your pitch. You have all the material written and completed, you have rehearsed it with your friends and enemies, and you have been working endlessly generating contacts. Now one of them agrees to see you. It's what you have worked toward: the pitch.

You have read up about how to handle a pitch and talked to your contacts and quizzed people about what to expect. Being the movie business, of course, a relatively simple business meeting has been blown up into something rather more dramatic. Although it is true that the outcome could mean an awful lot of money for the scriptwriter.

Some advisors have said that the writer should be emotional about the story, even to the point of making a fool of himself or herself. Some have even suggested that if a writer has difficulty in handling an audience, they should take acting classes. What it comes down to, yet again, is personality and what kind you may have. Of course, it also comes down to how hungry you are and how far you are prepared to go.

## Relying on the Log Line

There is no doubt about it, there are a lot of young people about and many of them seem to have a job that revolves around running a studio in Hollywood, or that's the way it appears. Along with youth comes the short attention span. There is no point sitting around bemoaning that fact, you just have to operate in a way that turns it to your advantage. A major factor in that endeavor is brevity, or keep it short with punch, or as Mr. Eastwood has said: "Cut to the chase."

These young folk don't have much truck with lengthy explanations, and as there is always someone chasing them to pitch a movie, their time is at a premium. Hence the idea of "concept" becomes essential, and you have to spend time learning and honing one of those in order to sell your script. There are concept guidelines: Tell your story and its hook in twenty-five words or less. This takes us back to the Hollywood staple: log line and outline.

**ALERT!**

Deals for screenplays, even actual films, are often made, believe it or not, on the basis of a few paragraphs—or, at most, on a short synopsis. It is said that the idea for the science fiction film *Outland* was sold on a log line: "It's High Noon in Outer Space."

A log line is the selling pitch that encapsulates the absolute essence of your story. (Tip: Don't use long words like "encapsulates" in your log line. It has too many syllables to it.) Another way of looking at the contents of a log line would be to visualize it as if it were in the poster for the picture. Naturally, these have a technical name, which came from the people who make the posters: One-Sheet.

You will see posters in frames on the walls of your local cinema, under "Coming Soon" or something like that. It's typical that the poster will have a picture of the lead actor(s) against a background that should give the viewer a good idea of the type of film being advertised. Then there might also be a line or two of type in the poster layout. It's that text that could have been your log line, although in reality, of course, had it been, the log line would have come a long time before the poster for the produced picture.

**QUESTION?**

**How do I know if my log line is any good?**
Only from the reactions of other people. Ask: "Excuse me, what does this say to you?" Then recite your log line. If you travel to work on a bus or train ask the person sitting next to you. (Be sure you look relatively respectable, and smile.) Note the reaction. If it's not what you want, write another log line. You'll be amazed how interested people will be.

Sometimes there will be log line–type text in newspaper advertisements. Generally, though, the text will be crowded out by quotes from reviews that are being used to promote the picture. Here are a few log line examples taken from actual film posters:

- *The Recruit* with Al Pacino: "Trust, Betrayal, Deception. In the C.I.A. Nothing Is What It Seems."
- *Murder by Numbers* with Sandra Bullock: "Let the Mind Games Begin."
- *Insomnia* with Al Pacino and Robin Williams: "Tough Cop. Brilliant Killer. Unspeakable Crime."
- *Dreamcatcher* with Morgan Freeman: "Four Friends Hang a Dreamcatcher in Their Cabin. It's About to Catch Something It Cannot Stop."

- *25th Hour* with Edward Norton: "Can You Change Your Whole Life in a Day?"
- *The Emperor's Club* with Kevin Kline: "In Everyone's Life There's That One Person Who Makes All the Difference."
- *Goldfinger* with Sean Connery: "Everything He Touches Turns to Excitement."

Keep in mind that those lines of text were written by professionals. When you come to write your log line, try to emulate the style of the professionals. Just as the poster was written and designed to entice people to want to see the picture, so your log line should be designed so that your audience, the Hollywood reader, is persuaded to read your spec script.

## Taking the Meeting

For the sake of simplicity, let's presume that the place of your meeting is in Los Angeles and that you live nearby. Let's also presume that you do not yet have an agent. This might be a good time to get yourself one if you can move quickly enough before the date of the meeting.

**ESSENTIAL**

You might want to take a look at *Breakfast at Tiffany's,* which has Audrey Hepburn looking her best. While the film itself may not be one of the greatest of all time, it does have a certain charm and style. Try to work out how you would pitch it at a meeting.

First of all, find out whom you will be pitching to. It probably won't be just one person; it'll be a small group. Establish what each person does and what their status is; in fact, find out as much as you can about them (including their ages). Take a page out of the salesman's manual: You are a golfer, so you always find out if your target is one. If the answer is yes, open your pitch with a golfing question.

Choose your wardrobe carefully; lean toward good quality casual.

Don't wear the chino/jeans uniform. Go for something more subtle. Pay attention to everything that is said.

This is where the personality aspects come into play. As the people at the meeting are going to be relatively sophisticated in the industry, or think they are, and you are not, they could have the upper hand; that's if you let them. They will look at you as the vulnerable member of the meeting because you are the person who wants something from them.

## Your Attitude

The essential attitude you have to have is one of serious nonchalance; give the impression that you don't really care so much about the outcome as you do about your script. In yourself, of course, you have it firmly established that this is a practice run. Do that and your attitude will reflect your inner feelings and you will emanate confidence.

If you keep your focus on the meeting being a rehearsal, you will better remember what is said. Way back in your memory bank recall that when Grace Kelly first went to Hollywood she knocked them out because she wore white gloves to a meeting; then they knew she was a lady. The main attribute you should exhibit is being a good listener. Concentrate on the others at the meeting, look them in the eyes, smile, and do not try to be clever.

What not to do at a meeting: don't sweat, swear, or come on to any of the participants. Do not try to appear cleverer than your hosts. Make your compliments subtle. For example: "Well, I thought, for instance, that *Gentle Pastures* had great style." (You had done your research and found out that one member of the team had green-lighted the film.)

## Don't Forget the "Meets" Line

The meets line is a shorthand frame-of-reference method of describing what a screenplay is about. This will give you an idea of the intellectual level your meeting may reach. Having said that, there is some value to the shorthand of, for example, *Spider-Man*-meets-*Sherlock Holmes*. The synergy of the two titles provides a metaphor for a possible meaning.

It may well happen that the term "meets line" will not even come up;

it's in fact becoming passé in some quarters. But it's obvious that you will be asked to describe what your spec screenplay is about. Even if the people at the meeting have read (glanced at or skimmed) your script, they will want to hear your take on it. You may learn that the meeting has been at the urging of a senior reader at the studio. If that's the case, brace yourself: the planets are favorable.

**FACT**

World-renowned director Fred Zinnemann (*High Noon, From Here to Eternity, The Day of the Jackal,* and many others) had a meeting in Hollywood when he was well past seventy. The thirty-year-old producer started by asking: "Tell me something about yourself." Apparently Mr. Zinnemann looked at the young man and said: "You go first."

## After the Meeting

The minute you get back from the meeting, whatever the outcome, make notes. Include attitudes, some of the more forceful questions posed by the members, what seemed to bug them, what seemed to please them. Get it firmly in mind that you were on an informational interview. You were in charge because nobody knew of your motivation. Now get ready for your next pitch and meeting.

## Chapter 21

E

**Working with an Agent**

The best way to succeed in Hollywood is to have a good agent who will help you make headway. There are a large number of agents in the business. Some of them are members of the AAR (Association of Author Representatives), which should mean—at least in theory—that they adhere to the morals, ethics, and business practices of the association. This chapter will help you find the right agent for you and avoid the crooks.

## The Agents

Agents are like salespeople who work on commission. If they get you a deal and sell your screenplay, they'll get a part of whatever you get from the studios—generally around 10 percent. That is why they are so picky about who they represent. If they see no chance of your work ever making it, they won't waste their time representing you.

However, if they do recognize your potential, they will do all the marketing, contracting, and negotiations for you, while you're free to begin writing another script. And if you are lucky, a good agent may also offer you advice; if any of them do, seriously consider taking it.

**QUESTION?**

**Will my agent advise me about my taxes?**
Not if he or she has any sense. It may well be that once you get high up the Hollywood ladder you might think your agent will take care of your life. This is not true, although your agent may well give you the name of a good accountant.

Agents aren't writers, but if they are any good they know what sells and how to sell it. Agents can be the making of your career and they can be the biggest pain, maybe both at the same time. Nevertheless, whatever you think of agents you are going to need one, unless you were brought up in the film industry and have a degree in law.

If you do not live in the Los Angeles or New York City areas, an agent is going to be essential. Actually, even if you do live there you are most certainly going to need one. You should understand a few things about the breed. They are commission-only salespeople. If any so-called agent asks for payments or fees in advance, be very wary and keep looking.

## The Managers

You can have both an agent and a manager or one or the other. Obviously, to have both is a fair indication that you might be doing quite well. Or it could mean that you will lose more money in commission, because a manager is paid on the same basis as the agent—the manager's cut is usually 15 percent, though rates do vary.

The theory about managers is that the service the client gets tends to be more personal, or at least that's what managers say. Many sit down with the client and draft out a plan of action that may cover one, two, or more years. Managers, more than most agents, will offer writing advice to their writers, which you might think is a good introduction to a business where other people tinkering with your material is the standard.

**FACT**

Agents and managers are emphatic that ageism is not part of their way of doing business. But what about the people actually buying the material? One writer was known to make a point of sending his young son to meetings. The older man would write the stuff, while the younger one took care of the face-to-face pitching.

## The Manager's Role

There's nothing wrong with managers hawking and selling a screenplay. However, they are supposed to have a lawyer on the phone when the negotiating is in progress. Obviously, the manager/writer relationship is a delicate one. But it can be a very valuable one because managers frequently handle the careers of directors. It doesn't take a brain surgeon to work out that having writers and directors in the same camp can prove to be synergistic.

# How to Find a Good Agent

Once you are hired or contracted to either sell your spec script or write one, it shouldn't be difficult to find an agent; after all, you will be handing them 10 percent of something. But what if you don't have a deal yet? It's still possible to find an agent even before you do any selling on your own.

The best way to find a good doctor, lawyer, dentist, or plumber is to have one recommended to you by a friend whose opinion you trust. It's the same with agents. However, the odds are that you don't have a friend who has an agent. And even if you did have one, some friends aren't too keen on recommending other friends to their agent; they tend to be possessive about them.

Those dear friends of yours will tell you such things as, "My agent has closed his/her books and isn't taking on any new clients." Do not despair—all is not lost. There are a number of reference books and Web sites you can research. (See Appendix B for details.) But before we move on to how you can find the right agent, there are a couple of things you should know.

## Reputable or Not?

No reputable agent would ever require payment other than for preapproved expenses. No self-respecting agent would ever charge reading or service fees, and most of the agents out there do abide by this unspoken rule. If your agent ever refers to another person or business that specializes in script doctoring, be aware that something shady may be going on. The most likely explanation is that the script doctor is your agent's cousin and needs an extra project to pay the bills.

**QUESTION?**

**What if I don't want to have an agent?**
That's fine, but there are drawbacks that could slow down your career. To start with, if an agent submits a screenplay, producers won't throw it into that luckless pile known as "unsolicited mail," so you'll get more attention for your script if you have an agent representing you.

## It's Time to Begin Your Search

Getting an agent is not easy. It would be lovely if all you had to do was to pick one from the reference books and put in a call. Unfortunately, it's going to take more effort than that. First of all, you should tackle the problem that even well-established writers have had to face: whether you want to work with a big-shot agent or one who's just starting out.

Would you prefer to be handled by one of the prestige giants like William Morris, who, it is argued, can use his clout because of the megastars he handles to push your product? A big-name agent like that has easy access at many studios and can certainly get your script seen, but will he have the time to do that? Or is he more likely to file it away and concentrate on his big-name clients, who are a sure bet when it comes to getting his commission?

On the other hand, a relatively unknown agent may have more of an interest in selling your screenplay and give you more attention. After all, he, too, is trying to make a name for himself in the business. But there are downsides as well. For one thing, an inexperienced agent may hurt rather than help a screenwriting career with just a few false moves. And in his eagerness for projects, a small-time agent may take on too many clients and end up with little time for each one.

You don't always get to pick your agent—it's hard enough just to find one—but keep in mind that settling for an agent that you're not happy with isn't the best course of action. Make sure that the agent you find is right for you, that you can work well together, and that you have at least some trust in what he's doing on your behalf.

## Hitting the Books

Let's say you have all the references books in front of you and you start going through them in an effort to find an agent you think might be good for you. It's a bit like picking racehorses. Some people like finding fun coincidences, while others begin with the letter A and go down from there.

What you should understand is that the entries in the reference books are based on information given to the publisher by the agent—that is, this isn't someone else's reference of the agent, it's what the agent chose to say about herself. This means that you won't see anything negative—but you'll also get lots of valuable information that you should pay attention to. For instance, if the entry tells you the agent doesn't handle animation, don't waste her time and yours by sending her an outline of your updated version of *Snow White and the Seven Dwarfs*.

What you can do is check the entry against the agent's name where it says when the agency was established. If it's 1952, obviously the outfit has been around for a fair time; if it's 2002, that's a different matter. You might presume that the longer-established agency has wiser agents and a longer credit list of successes. On the other hand, the young one might be better for you; maybe the agents in the newer agency are hip and cool and eager to prove themselves in the industry.

## Working the Phones

Agents are generally available on the phone, except for the superagents who tend to be snooty and unavailable. Nevertheless, it would be a good idea to start calling around when you begin looking for representation. Do not presume you are going to have a heart-to-heart chat with an agent about your career. Try that and you will find the call has come to a sudden end; agents are busy people.

What can get you into a conversation is to say to the agent or her assistant/secretary that you are a new scriptwriter seeking representation and inquire whether they are taking on new clients. The standard reply is that yes, they always consider new talent. This will be followed by a request that you send in a query letter and an outline.

**ESSENTIAL**

Agents would strongly prefer writers seeking representation to inquire with them alone. Don't take any notice; it frequently takes a month or longer for an agent to send a form letter back rejecting your request. Would you want to wait a year for twelve agents to say no?

But you might hit them on a slow day and they could ask you what your project is about. Bingo, now you have a chance to talk about your work. Don't start going off on an hour-long lecture—just give them your log line and the first paragraph you worked so hard on, and see where the conversation takes you. Chances are it will end up with the same query letter/outline request.

What you accomplish by telling the agent about your work is that you have increased the chances of having your material read instead of languishing in the pending/unsolicited file—after all, it's now been requested. So when you send in that letter, be sure you have the person's name—spelled correctly—and address your query letter to him or her personally; make reference to your telephone conversation. To be on the safe side, print "Requested Material" on the outside of the envelope.

## The Query Letter

Even if you don't get that personal conversation, sending a query letter is still a well-established method. Keep your query letter to a page and forget any funny stuff designed to get the reader's attention, like colors, drawings, and smart-aleck remarks. If you were an agent, how many pages of a query letter would you have time to plow through? Not too many, if you could help it.

The query letter should contain a brief cover letter that will mention your pertinent career accomplishments and the purpose of your writing. To the cover letter, you will attach the outline or treatment and a self-addressed stamped envelope, so that the agent may send you a reply.

Aspiring screenwriters should set aside a part of every day to network, either on the telephone or the computer. The Internet is an amazing source. Just be selective with the material you access; not everyone who has a Web site is a saint.

If you find that you aren't getting any positive responses to your query letters, there a few simple factors that might be holding you back: Do you make sure that the agent you are addressing is still with the agency where you are sending your query letter? Agents move around in the industry and that agent may have gone elsewhere. Do you write to "Dear Agent," instead of finding out the correct name? Do you take care to spell the agent's name correctly? Do you tell the potential agent what a wonderful writer you are?

Any one of these mistakes will get a writer a rejection slip. It may be that it is not the fault of the agent but of the writer that is causing all the rejections. There is a proper and an improper way of doing business that comes before an agent gets down to reading a spec screenplay. Make sure you aren't shortchanging yourself.

# Once You Have an Agent

When you actually get an agent, keep in mind that first there's the honeymoon; so now when you go to cocktail parties you can make remarks like, "Yeah, well, according to my agent. . . . " Having an agent puts you up a few rungs in the industry. However, it will be your work that will keep you there and with hope will cement your relationship with your agent, so that the honeymoon turns out to be a long-term arrangement.

And it's important not to forget that the agent/writer relationship should always remain a business relationship, and that each one of you should have your best interests in mind, especially when it comes to paying your agent commission.

## Contract and Commission

The agent's income today is calculated at the rate of 10 percent of whatever they sell, which is less than literary agents, who earn 15 percent (the rate goes up to 20 percent if foreign manuscript sales are involved). If they don't do it themselves, many literary agents have correspondent agents who handle film sales. The rule of thumb is that generally the size of the agency will dictate their involvement, and the degree of it, in film sales. Film agents who belong to the Society of Authors' Representatives are prohibited from charging more than 10 percent commission.

The contract between an author and an agent typically contains a clause that the agent collects money on behalf of the writer. The agent then takes his commission before passing on the rest of the money to the writer. You might ask: Why doesn't the author get paid in full, then pay his or her agent the commission? One reason might be that authors can be funny people who can come up with all sorts of reasons why the agent isn't worth the commission. The authors in those cases tend to conveniently forget that without the agent they wouldn't have a sale. All of which makes it very clear why the agent should collect the money and pay the author.

Most agent/writer contracts have a clause where each can give a three-month termination notice. Agents typically want new clients to sign for a specified period—six months to a year is not unusual. If an agent isn't getting anywhere after three months, they tend to cool off. Tip: Never bug your agent.

Another question might be: Supposing the agent does get paid, then takes off for some island in the Pacific with all my money? Seeing that such action is a big-time offense and would ruin an agent's career, to say nothing of possible incarceration, it's highly unlikely to happen. There is an alternative if you are paranoid, and that's to work with an entertainment attorney. Some lawyers work by the hour, in which case the writer would receive the money and the lawyer would bill the writer for the hours worked.

It is not unusual for agents and production companies to request that the writer sign a release form before they will accept a script for a reading. This is to protect them from nuisance lawsuits. Essentially, the release says you own the material and have the right to offer it for sale. It also says you will not sue if the agent/company has a similar script in development.

## What If You Don't Get an Agent?

Not having an agent is not exactly the end to your career in the cinema world. However, if possible you should try and avoid this situation. Not having an agent means you have to sell your work yourself, and that's precious time away from writing. If you spend the time it takes to get to know and negotiate the film industry, you might just as well give up writing and become an agent yourself.

It's probably fair to say that the writers who don't end up with an agent either have given up trying to get one or they are really not all that good at what they do. It can be heartbreaking because it's a form of deep rejection: Here you have been working on something that might well be a part of you and now these agents are turning up their noses. It's when writers get into this situation that they become prey for the script editors and other fee-charging advisors.

## Beware the Fee-Charging Agent

The first red flag that signifies someone is after your money and not your ability to write screenplays is when a reply comes back to a standard submission and query: "We thought what you sent us had strong possibilities. However, like a lot of screenplays circulating today, it does need some polishing. We would suggest . . . ." It's your wallet they want to polish, not your screenplay. The trouble is compounded if you bite and get involved with these people; the fees due will keep piling up along with the edits.

## Becoming an Agent

There's always a bright side. If you can't find an agent, why not become one yourself? You'll gains tons of experience in the industry, make a few sales, and then—who knows?—maybe the experience will teach you how you can improve your own work. Then, you can one day give up your agenting career and go back to screenwriting.

Imagine you are an agent. You might work in one of the classy and very large outfits in an upscale Beverly Hills office, or you might work out of your home. Essentially, wherever you work, you do the same thing: evaluate properties and try to sell them. That, of course, is an oversimplification, but no matter how you dress it up, it's very close to the bottom line of the job.

Basically anyone can become an agent; all they have to do if they live and operate in California is to become licensed and bonded with the State Labor Commission. (Other states have similar regulations.) While not a requirement, it is important to the client that the agent is a WGA (Writers Guild of America) signatory. Wherever you live, check the qualifications, memberships, and whatever state licensing requirements are in force.

**ALERT!**

A good agent will know by the first ten or fifteen pages of a spec screenplay if it's worthwhile to keep going. The story may be attractive, the structure fair, but the real killer will be the dialogue. If the dialogue is flat, clichéd, and uninteresting, that will be that. Move on to the next script.

The most important part of being an agent is knowing the industry—and making sure that the industry knows you. It's fairly typical that new agents are spinoffs from other larger agencies and often bring existing clients with them. In publishing it's common for editors to turn to being agents; the money is better. It stands to reason that for any agent to be a success, they have to be connected; this is particularly so in Hollywood.

An agent is only as good as her reputation, and she builds a reputation by discovering winners. That's why agents are so picky about taking on new clients and their work. The worst thing an agent can do is to send a studio a clunker of a script with a buildup that trumpets it's the next *Die Hard* when it's really a sad knockoff. The agent vouches for the integrity of each script he or she represents. (E)

## Chapter 22

# The Screenwriter's Future

Trying to predict the future of anyone, let alone a scriptwriter, is an awesome task and probably a thankless one. Scriptwriters are faced with a major problem, which is that everyone thinks he or she can write. If you asked the odd movie executive if he could play the violin, he'd probably laugh and tell you of course not, it would take years to learn how to play the violin. But at the drop of a page a movie executive will tell a scriptwriter how to write.

# A Screenwriter's Life

There is a very nice middle-aged lady who lives in a good-sized cabin in the middle of the High Sierras in California with her dog. This lady happens to be an excellent screenwriter. She doesn't drink very much, she gave up smoking and loud men, and she gets on very well with her two grown-up children. When people meet her for the first time they find it hard to believe what she does for a living.

If you were to create a scriptwriter as a character for your film, it's doubtful if he or she would fit this image. Well, not all Italians are in the Mafia either. A screenwriter can have a wonderful life; the work is very rewarding, the pay—when it comes—is pretty good, too; and you can meet some very interesting people in this line of work.

A Hollywood trade paper, *Hollywood Scriptwriter,* publishes a survey every August with listings of WGA agencies that are open to submissions from readers. The periodical covers the industry in general, including Web site reviews.

## A "Real" Screenwriter

Many people wonder what a "real" screenwriter looks like and where these people live. The odd thing is, most screenwriters are probably very much like you. Sure, there are a few who live in Hollywood, drink too much, have wild parties, and are constantly surrounded by film industry people, but this isn't the case for everyone.

However, there are some distinctions that are common to those of the screenwriting profession. Imagination, inquisitiveness, and open-mindedness, though they are becoming rarer, are the traits of the best screenwriters. Screenwriters seek after realism, and many are inspired by an urge to comment on the human condition, coupled with a need to seek out the original and tell a good story.

You may think that it takes years to earn the title of screenwriter, but screenwriting careers are made in Hollywood every day. Screenplay acceptances and contracts *do* happen, to first-timers as well as experienced writers—but you've got to make them happen. It will take a huge amount of work as well as determination, patience, and, in some cases, luck, but the opportunities are there—you just have to seize them. Once you do, your biggest worry will be how to deal with all that good fortune and success.

**FACT**

William Faulkner, an American novelist who tried his hand at screenwriting, had this to say about the craft: "Everything goes by the board: honor, pride, decency . . . to get the screenplay written. If a writer had to rob his mother, he will not hesitate; *Citizen Kane* is worth any number of old ladies."

## Living with Success

Screenwriters must be careful about success and failure; a strong reaction to either one can destroy a career and even a life. Celebrity is to be avoided at all costs; that comes easier to writers than many others, because the genuine ones don't need to be known. Like many of the very good they are always uncertain of their talent; they have learned the value of humility.

More than anything they are grateful that they have found a way to write that rewards them not only in the way they might have thought when they started out, with money, but with the knowledge that the best in everything is simplicity. The best writer is a simple soul aiming to please, which might be why it is easy to take advantage of writers. It was written that the pen is mightier than the sword. Wield it well if you can.

## Dealing with Rejection

Of course, the flip side of success and celebrity is rejection. As the statistics combed from the literature of psychoanalysts tell us, rejection is a big number in the mental health problem department. Unfortunately, when you are a writer of any kind, rejection is part and parcel of the game. If in times of stress you are attracted to high places like the Golden Gate Bridge, perhaps you should consider another line of work. Even if you think you can handle rejection, always remember that people judging your work are totally subjective and their rejection may have less to do with the actual script than with a number of other factors, some of which have nothing to do with you.

## Learning from Rejection

When it comes to rejection, the only thing you can do is learn from it. If you get form rejections, it's still worth the effort to call the agents/producers and in a charming manner ask if on your next submission they could kindly offer some advice along with their rejection. You'll be surprised at their reaction.

**ESSENTIAL**

Try to form a screenwriter's group. Aim to have four or five members—keep the membership low and try to find serious people. If it's possible, arrange to meet at each other's homes every two weeks or so. Make it plain that the group welcomes honest opinions, but that courtesy should be kept.

A modern playwright of some renown has said that he never sends in a play to be read, he always "performs" it. In fact, not one of his plays that have been on Broadway got anywhere with a producer until he "performed" it. That's worth thinking about. At the risk of boring some of your friends, you might try out your screenplay by reading it to them. The other advantage to "performing" your screenplays, even to an audience of one (you), is that you will get to know how it "plays."

## What the Critics Say

Even if your script is accepted by the studio for production, there is another form of rejection—one that is more public and arguably more difficult to deal with. It's the rejection of the film critic or film reviewer, who proclaims a film as a failure.

If anyone wants to judge the effectiveness of critics, think of the many times one has praised a film as Oscar potential and when you came out of the cinema after seeing it you wondered if the critic was talking about the same film. This isn't to say the critic was wrong, only that you and the critic didn't get the same message from the picture.

Once you've had your screenplay accepted and it is in production, there will come the day when it is released (some might say "escaped"), and the reviews of it hit the newsstands. While you may be a stoic sort of person, completely well balanced and not subject to self-doubt and self-recrimination, these reviews, nevertheless, can have a tremendous effect. Not so much on your current well-being, but on your Hollywood future.

**FACT**

According to Christopher Keane, novelist and screenwriter, "In Hollywood, the story gets you in the door. The first question a producer asks is not who the movie's about but what it's about. . . . Without a strong story to guide them, your characters, though they may be fully developed, will wander aimlessly around until the producer yawns and thanks you for your time."

## A Screenwriter's Income

It's not unreasonable to have some idea of how much you might be paid for writing something that could end up being used in a film or television production. The trouble is that, like a lot of things, only the most extravagant tales reach the columns of the newspapers.

Most people have read an item that says so and so was paid some extraordinary amount of money for scripting such and such a film and when is all this gross-flowing river of money ever going to stop? Well, for most scriptwriters it never started.

## Minimum Wage

While there is no minimum wage laid out, the WGA does publish the WGA Theatrical and Television Basic Agreement, which includes a section on "Theatrical Compensation." Original screenplay and treatment travels from a recommended low of nearly $50,000 to a high of about $100,000.

In addition to the Basic Agreement there is also something called the WGA Low Budget Agreement Fact Sheet. It may not apply to you, but you never know; however, it does give you another yardstick against which to judge what you may be offered.

The first two points read:

1. The Low Budget Agreement is offered to WGA members and nonmembers for purchases of existing screenplays and one rewrite. It is not for development.
2. The agreement applies to films budgeted at $750,000 and below.

**ALERT!**

One way to keep your mind on possible film ideas is to write down your dreams as soon as you wake up (keep your journal and a pen right by your bed). When you think about your dreams later, you may find an interesting idea beckoning.

From that point onward it is suggested that you call your lawyer. It should be noted that a freelance scriptwriter is generally classified by the IRS as a self-employed person. Of course, this may not apply to you, but either way it might be prudent to consult your local IRS advisor, who can tell you about nasty things like self-employment tax and what sort of genuine expenses you can claim.

## Development Deals

Sometimes a writer is offered a development deal, or step deal. This means that the scriptwriter receives an advance, then more money as he or she moves through the script-development stages step by step. It is not uncommon for the process to grind to a halt. When that happens, you are said to be "mired in development hell."

There have been many writers who have made a very good living out of writing scripts that go through the development process only to end up as scrapped projects. In such cases, the advance is the writer's consolation prize for the time and effort spent on writing the screenplay that will never make it to the silver screen.

**FACT**

Every spacecraft that zooms away from a planet about to implode, every monster that wields a bloody axe, every gun that spouts bullets, every fire that consumes buildings, every miracle that saves a life, every laugh that warms a soul, every hero who rides into the valley and every villain who leaves; all of these emanate from the pen of the screenwriter.

## Script Doctors

In Hollywood there are veteran writers who are well known for being experts in certain elements of a screenplay, such as dialogue, action, love scenes, and so on. These writers have built reputations writing in the same limited vein over and over. They aren't asked to write action if they have the reputation for writing dialogue, or the other way around. Basically, they are specialists, and they are sometimes called upon by the studios to fix a script that is lacking in one area.

These writers, known as *script doctors*, do exactly what their job title implies—they fix the parts of the script that aren't done right, doctoring the flow, dialogue, scene structure, and so forth. Script doctoring can be a highly paid occupation; many of them earn more than real doctors.

If you are better at editing than creating original work, you may consider script doctoring as an alternative career option. Of course, the screenplays you'd work on would never carry your name, but you'd get a lot more projects that actually make it to the screen, and you'll get valuable experience along the way.

## Directing Your Own Screenplay

If a writer is working with a studio and/or a producer or director, then he or she will have to learn the art of compromise. There is only one situation where the scriptwriter can have anything approaching control and that's if he or she directs the film as well as writes it.

Many writers work toward directing, even though in the early days directors were looked on as technicians, certainly not artists. It was the French who changed that opinion when they proposed their principle of the auteur. (Woody Allen is a good example of an American auteur.) In spite of that, there are many highly experienced and talented writers who hold to the opinion that almost anyone in the business can do what a director does. However, very few directors can do what the people they control do: cinematographers, editors, sound editors, to name only three of the most important. Ⓔ

*Appendix A*

# Glossary

When it comes to screenwriting, it helps to know the lingo. You can use the following glossary to see how much you already know and brush up on the terms that you may have forgotten.

**action:** The text in the script that appears flush left and provides background information as well as the action taking place on the screen. This text should be concise and refer to what the audience would see and hear.

**back story:** Information about a character's past that helps viewers to better understand the story.

**conflict:** In terms of the screenplay, conflict provides tension and builds the dramatic action, leading up to confrontation and eventually resolution.

**copyright:** Legal ownership of written material, including the right of reproduction.

**crisis:** A point in the plot when two or more forces confront each other.

**denouement:** The period that follows the climax, when any remaining issues are resolved.

**dramatic action:** The progression of the plot that drives the story line through the plot points and on to a resolution.

**exposition:** The parts of a script that show what happened previously and identify the characters and the time and place of the action. Exposition shouldn't be spelled out by the characters but be an invisible part of the story.

**genre:** Film category such as drama, comedy, and action. Many genres may be subdivided into subgenres—comedy may be a romantic comedy, slapstick, or a parody.

**Hollywood:** A town in southern California, Hollywood has become a catch-all term for the American film industry.

**Indie:** Independent filmmaker, studio, or producer; indies generally have smaller budgets and frequently make films that are considered "artsy" as opposed to commercial or mainstream.

**log line:** A compelling one-liner or two-line description of a screenplay that will help you sell your idea.

**master scene:** All the action and dialogue that occurs within one setting at a particular time.

**"meets" line:** A one-liner that describes a film by using the "meets" formula—for instance, you may describe a new frat house comedy with the following "meets" line: *"Animal House* meets *There's Something About Mary."*

**parenthetical:** In a script, a word or phrase in parentheses between the character's name and the dialogue line, which provides information about how the dialogue is spoken.

**plot:** What happens in the movie.

**plot point:** A particular occurrence within a script when something happens to change the direction of the story.

**prop:** An object used by the actors in a scene; one of the most common props in today's movies is the phone.

**scenario:** See *shooting script.*

**scene:** One event in a screenplay, with a beginning, a middle, and an end; a scene often contains a crisis or confrontation, and always advances the story.

**scene transition:** In the script, you move from scene to scene by way of a scene transition, set in all caps and appearing in the right margin; your basic options with scene transition are DISSOLVE TO, CUT TO, and FADE TO BLACK.

**shooting script:** A detailed script written for film production (particularly the director and camera crew), it includes camera shots and other material not appropriate for the spec script.

**slug line:** Identifies the time and location of a scene. INT. (interior) and EXT. (exterior) indicate whether the scene is taking place inside or outside. NIGHT or DAY indicate the time of day. For example: INT. LIVING ROOM – NIGHT. The slug line information is always given in capital letters.

**spec script:** The basic form of a script used to sell the film idea; unlike a shooting script, it does not contain shooting details like camera angles.

**storyboard:** Sketches of a script's scenes that the director uses to plan the making of the film.

**subtext:** The thoughts and motivations that influence the characters, even though they are never directly expressed.

**synopsis:** Detailed outline of the film, scene by scene, but without the dialogue.

**three-act structure:** Most film scripts (as well as theater plays) may be divided into three acts; the first act introduces the story and character, the second act moves the story forward through the plot points and develops the characters, and the third act provides the resolution.

**treatment:** A breakdown of a story that describes it in just a few pages. Often a producer who is considering a script will ask to have a treatment written to sell him or her on the story.

**voice-over (V.O.):** Commentary by a character or narrator that is heard from off-screen or that is set up as a character's thoughts.

## Appendix B

# Additional Resources

Now that you've completed this book, don't forget that there are other resources available to you. From Web sites and chat forums to books and magazines, there is a wealth of information out there—as long as you know where to look.

# Further Reading

Biskind, Peter. *Easy Riders, Raging Bulls: How the Sex-Drugs-and-Rock 'n' Roll Generation Saved Hollywood.* (New York: Simon & Schuster, 1999).

Crowe, Cameron. *Conversations with Wilder.* (New York: Alfred A. Knopf, 1999).

Field, Syd. *Screenplay: The Foundations of Screenwriting.* Third edition. (Fine Publications, 1994).

Field, Syd. *Four Screenplays: Studies in the American Screenplay.* (New York: Dell Trade Paperback, 1994).

Hampe, Barry. *Making Documentary Films and Reality Videos.* (New York: Owl Books., 1997).

Harmetz, Aljean. *The Making of Casablanca: Bogart, Bergman, and World War II.* (New York: Hyperion Books, 2002).

Iglesias, Karl. *The 101 Habits of Highly Successful Screenwriters: Insider's Secrets from Hollywood's Top Writers.* (Avon, MA: Adams Media Corporation, 2001).

Keane, Christopher. *How to Write a Selling Screenplay: A Step-by-Step Approach to Developing Your Story and Writing Your Screenplay by One of Today's Most Successful Screenwriters and Teachers.* (New York: Bantam Doubleday Dell Publication, 1998).

Litwak, Mark. *Reel Power: The Struggle for Influence and Success in the New Hollywood.* (Los Angeles: Silman-James Press, 1994).

O'Donnell, Pierce and Dennis McDougal. *Fatal Subtraction. How Hollywood Really Does Business.* (New York: Doubleday, 1992).

Parkinson, David. *History of Film.* (New York: Thames and Hudson, Inc., 1996).

Salamon, Julie. *The Devil's Candy. The Anatomy of a Hollywood Fiasco.* (Cambridge, MA: DaCapo Press, 2002).

Straczynski, Michael J. *The Complete Book of Scriptwriting.* (Cincinnati, Ohio: Writer's Digest Books, 2002).

Trottier, David *The Screenwriter's Bible: A Complete Guide to Writing, Formatting, and Selling Your Script.* Third Edition. (Los Angeles, CA: Silman-James Press, 1998).

Wilder, Billy. *Double Indemnity: The Complete Screenplay.* (Berkeley, CA: University of California Press, 2000).

Wilder, Billy. *Sunset Boulevard: The Complete Screenplay.* (Berkeley, CA: University of California Press, 1999).

Wilen, Lydia and Joan Wilen. *How to Sell Your Screenplay: A Realistic Guide to Getting a Television or Film Deal.* (New York: Square One Publishers, 2001).

Winokur, Jon. *Writers on Writing.* Third edition. (Philadelphia, PA: Running Press Book Publishers, 1990).

# Periodicals

### Daily Variety
5700 Wilshire Blvd, Suite 120
Los Angeles, CA 90036
(323) 857-6600
*www.variety.com*

### The Hollywood Reporter
5055 Wilshire Blvd.
Los Angeles, CA 90036
(323) 525-2000
*www.hollywoodreporter.com*

### Hollywood Scriptwriter
P.O. Box 10277
Burbank, CA 91510
*www.hollywoodscriptwriter.com*

# Professional Organizations

### Writers Guild of America, East
555 West 55th Street, Suite 1230
New York, NY 10019-2967
(212) 767-7800
*www.wgaeast.org*

### Writers Guild of America, West
7000 West 3rd Street
Los Angeles, CA 90048-4329
(323) 951-4000
*www.wga.org*

### U.S. Copyright Office
Library of Congress
101 Independence Avenue, SE
Washington, DC 20559-6000
(202) 707-3000 (Information)

### Academy of Motion Picture Arts and Sciences
8949 Wilshire Blvd
Beverly Hills, CA 90211-1972
(310) 247-3000
*www.oscars.org*

# Screenwriting Software

### Final Draft
16000 Ventura Blvd., Suite 800
Encino, CA 91436
(800) 231-4055
*www.finaldraft.com*

### The Writer's Store
2040 Westwood Blvd.
Los Angeles, CA 90025
(866) 229-7483
*www.writersstore.com*

### Screentalk
*www.screentalk.biz*

*Appendix C*

# Sample Materials

This appendix contains sample materials for the film *Loophole*, including the treatment, screenplay cover page, and sample scene, which you may use for your reference.

## Sample Treatment

**LOOPHOLE**

**A Treatment**

**Robert Pollock**

**The Bank That Couldn't Be Robbed**

Robert Pollock

ADDRESS

PHONE NUMBER

**Cockney Mike Daniels**, an ace thief and master safe-cracker has a major, fail-safe, plan: how to crack an uncrackable vault in an unrobbable London bank and get away with millions.

He finds **Stephen Booker,** an out-of-work architect and civil engineer, whose comfortable suburban life is coming apart, including his marriage. He picks his brains, wears down his moral resistance, and hires him.

Then he puts together a band of five expert thieves, and lays out his plan: to go down into the London sewers under the bank, negotiate the black, rat-infested waters, and tunnel up into the vault.

**Stephen Booker** demonstrates his expert contribution to the plan, which is superbly detailed.

They have one weekend to do the job. The vault door has a time lock. It won't function until the opening of business Monday morning. In that time frame the group has to dig a tunnel under the vault, bore up into the floor of the vault, and blast open a way in.

There is the constant danger of lethal gas in the tunnel. **Booker** discovers that Daniels has concealed diving equipment stashed; if it rains outside on the London streets, the sewers will flood.

The alarms sound, the police arrive. As there is no

sign above in the bank of a forced entry, they mount a surveillance and wait. Down inside the vault the robbery goes on. The rains come and the tunnel starts to flood.

**Booker** decides to stay and risk the flood; the water is slowly rising to the top of the tunnel. **Daniels** puts his diving equipment on. The others in the sewer are frantically swimming away in an effort to get to a way out and climb up to a manhole cover at street level.

At a sewage pumping station down from the bank, a screen filter stops large pieces of debris from fouling up the works. A technician inspects the filter screen. He sees the matted head of a man floating in the sewage. (There is a time transition.)

A moving van at the driveway to a suburban house is being loaded. A woman, **Stephen Booker's wife**, sees the postman coming up the drive. She goes to meet him and takes the mail. She looks through the mail and studies a postcard of a beach. She calls into the house:  Darling, who do we know in Australia?

ENDS.

# Sample Screenplay Cover Page

LOOPHOLE

by

Robert Pollock

Registered WGAw No.xxxxx                    street address

                                            city, state, zip

                                            phone number

©Robert Pollock YEAR                        e-mail address

# Sample Scene

```
INT.  WAREHOUSE   LONDON   NIGHT
```

MIKE DANIELS is crouched over a large SAFE. A thin beam of light cuts through the blackness to show the keyhole of the safe.

A THIN MAN holds a FLASHLIGHT. A short FAT MAN stands by a window that is covered by black felt. A BLACK CAT is crouching low over the floor; its tail lashes in anger.

Daniels feeds a DETONATOR into the keyhole and tapes it.

> DANIELS
> That should do it. You can cover up now.

He watches the THIN MAN covering the door of the safe.

> DANIELS
> Funny stuff, nitro. You got to watch it.
> Like fat men, it sweats with old age.

The THIN MAN steps away from the safe. Daniels goes to it and trails detonator wire across the floor into an office.

                              DANIELS
        Right, then.


    The three men crouch behind a desk in the office. There
is a muffled ROAR. A filing-cabinet drawer slides open.
The cat SCREECHES, jumps in the air, and runs out of
sight.

    The three men smile at each other.

# Index

# THE EVERYTHING SERIES!

## BUSINESS & PERSONAL FINANCE

Everything® Budgeting Book
Everything® Business Planning Book
Everything® Coaching and Mentoring Book
Everything® Fundraising Book
Everything® Get Out of Debt Book
Everything® Grant Writing Book
Everything® Home-Based Business Book
Everything® Homebuying Book, 2nd Ed.
Everything® Homeselling Book, 2nd Ed.
Everything® Investing Book, 2nd Ed.
Everything® Landlording Book
Everything® Leadership Book
Everything® Managing People Book
Everything® Negotiating Book
Everything® Online Business Book
Everything® Personal Finance Book
Everything® Personal Finance in Your 20s
    and 30s Book
Everything® Project Management Book
Everything® Real Estate Investing Book
Everything® Robert's Rules Book, $7.95
Everything® Selling Book
Everything® Start Your Own Business Book
Everything® Wills & Estate Planning Book

## COOKING

Everything® Barbecue Cookbook
Everything® Bartender's Book, $9.95
Everything® Chinese Cookbook
Everything® Cocktail Parties and Drinks
    Book
Everything® College Cookbook
Everything® Cookbook
Everything® Cooking for Two Cookbook
Everything® Diabetes Cookbook
Everything® Easy Gourmet Cookbook
Everything® Fondue Cookbook
Everything® Gluten-Free Cookbook

Everything® Grilling Cookbook
Everything® Healthy Meals in Minutes
    Cookbook
Everything® Holiday Cookbook
Everything® Indian Cookbook
Everything® Italian Cookbook
Everything® Low-Carb Cookbook
Everything® Low-Fat High-Flavor Cookbook
Everything® Low-Salt Cookbook
Everything® Meals for a Month Cookbook
Everything® Mediterranean Cookbook
Everything® Mexican Cookbook
Everything® One-Pot Cookbook
Everything® Pasta Cookbook
Everything® Quick Meals Cookbook
Everything® Slow Cooker Cookbook
Everything® Slow Cooking for a Crowd
    Cookbook
Everything® Soup Cookbook
Everything® Thai Cookbook
Everything® Vegetarian Cookbook
Everything® Wine Book, 2nd Ed.

## CRAFT SERIES

Everything® Crafts—Baby Scrapbooking
Everything® Crafts—Bead Your Own Jewelry
Everything® Crafts—Create Your Own
    Greeting Cards
Everything® Crafts—Easy Projects
Everything® Crafts—Polymer Clay for
    Beginners
Everything® Crafts—Rubber Stamping
    Made Easy
Everything® Crafts—Wedding Decorations
    and Keepsakes

## HEALTH

Everything® Alzheimer's Book
Everything® Diabetes Book
Everything® Health Guide to Controlling
    Anxiety

Everything® Hypnosis Book
Everything® Low Cholesterol Book
Everything® Massage Book
Everything® Menopause Book
Everything® Nutrition Book
Everything® Reflexology Book
Everything® Stress Management Book

## HISTORY

Everything® American Government Book
Everything® American History Book
Everything® Civil War Book
Everything® Irish History & Heritage Book
Everything® Middle East Book

## HOBBIES & GAMES

Everything® Blackjack Strategy Book
Everything® Brain Strain Book, $9.95
Everything® Bridge Book
Everything® Candlemaking Book
Everything® Card Games Book
Everything® Card Tricks Book, $9.95
Everything® Cartooning Book
Everything® Casino Gambling Book, 2nd Ed.
Everything® Chess Basics Book
Everything® Craps Strategy Book
Everything® Crossword and Puzzle Book
Everything® Crossword Challenge Book
Everything® Cryptograms Book, $9.95
Everything® Digital Photography Book
Everything® Drawing Book
Everything® Easy Crosswords Book
Everything® Family Tree Book, 2nd Ed.
Everything® Games Book, 2nd Ed.
Everything® Knitting Book
Everything® Knots Book
Everything® Photography Book
Everything® Poker Strategy Book
Everything® Pool & Billiards Book
Everything® Quilting Book
Everything® Scrapbooking Book

All Everything® books are priced at $12.95 or $14.95, unless otherwise stated. Prices subject to change without notice.

Everything® Sewing Book
Everything® Test Your IQ Book, $9.95
Everything® Travel Crosswords Book, $9.95
Everything® Woodworking Book
Everything® Word Games Challenge Book
Everything® Word Search Book

## HOME IMPROVEMENT

Everything® Feng Shui Book
Everything® Feng Shui Decluttering Book,
    $9.95
Everything® Fix-It Book
Everything® Homebuilding Book
Everything® Lawn Care Book
Everything® Organize Your Home Book

## EVERYTHING® KIDS' BOOKS

**All titles are $6.95**
Everything® Kids' Animal Puzzle & Activity
    Book
Everything® Kids' Baseball Book, 3rd Ed.
Everything® Kids' Bible Trivia Book
Everything® Kids' Bugs Book
Everything® Kids' Christmas Puzzle
    & Activity Book
Everything® Kids' Cookbook
Everything® Kids' Crazy Puzzles Book
Everything® Kids' Dinosaurs Book
Everything® Kids' Gross Jokes Book
Everything® Kids' Gross Puzzle and
    Activity Book
Everything® Kids' Halloween Puzzle
    & Activity Book
Everything® Kids' Hidden Pictures Book
Everything® Kids' Joke Book
Everything® Kids' Knock Knock Book
Everything® Kids' Math Puzzles Book
Everything® Kids' Mazes Book
Everything® Kids' Money Book
Everything® Kids' Nature Book
Everything® Kids' Puzzle Book
Everything® Kids' Riddles & Brain Teasers Book
Everything® Kids' Science Experiments Book
Everything® Kids' Sharks Book
Everything® Kids' Soccer Book
Everything® Kids' Travel Activity Book

## KIDS' STORY BOOKS

Everything® Fairy Tales Book

## LANGUAGE

Everything® Conversational Japanese Book
    (with CD), $19.95
Everything® French Phrase Book, $9.95
Everything® French Verb Book, $9.95
Everything® Inglés Book
Everything® Learning French Book
Everything® Learning German Book
Everything® Learning Italian Book
Everything® Learning Latin Book
Everything® Learning Spanish Book
Everything® Sign Language Book
Everything® Spanish Grammar Book
Everything® Spanish Practice Book
    (with CD), $19.95
Everything® Spanish Phrase Book, $9.95
Everything® Spanish Verb Book, $9.95

## MUSIC

Everything® Drums Book (with CD), $19.95
Everything® Guitar Book
Everything® Home Recording Book
Everything® Playing Piano and Keyboards
    Book
Everything® Reading Music Book (with CD),
    $19.95
Everything® Rock & Blues Guitar Book
    (with CD), $19.95
Everything® Songwriting Book

## NEW AGE

Everything® Astrology Book, 2nd Ed.
Everything® Dreams Book, 2nd Ed.
Everything® Ghost Book
Everything® Love Signs Book, $9.95
Everything® Numerology Book
Everything® Paganism Book
Everything® Palmistry Book
Everything® Psychic Book
Everything® Reiki Book
Everything® Tarot Book
Everything® Wicca and Witchcraft Book

## PARENTING

Everything® Baby Names Book
Everything® Baby Shower Book
Everything® Baby's First Food Book
Everything® Baby's First Year Book
Everything® Birthing Book
Everything® Breastfeeding Book
Everything® Father-to-Be Book
Everything® Father's First Year Book
Everything® Get Ready for Baby Book
Everything® Get Your Baby to Sleep Book,
    $9.95
Everything® Getting Pregnant Book
Everything® Homeschooling Book
Everything® Mother's First Year Book
Everything® Parent's Guide to Children
    and Divorce
Everything® Parent's Guide to Children
    with ADD/ADHD
Everything® Parent's Guide to Children
    with Asperger's Syndrome
Everything® Parent's Guide to Children
    with Autism
Everything® Parent's Guide to Children with
    Bipolar Disorder
Everything® Parent's Guide to Children
    with Dyslexia
Everything® Parent's Guide to Positive
    Discipline
Everything® Parent's Guide to Raising a
    Successful Child
Everything® Parent's Guide to Tantrums
Everything® Parent's Guide to the Overweight
    Child
Everything® Parent's Guide to the Strong-
    Willed Child
Everything® Parenting a Teenager Book
Everything® Potty Training Book, $9.95
Everything® Pregnancy Book, 2nd Ed.
Everything® Pregnancy Fitness Book
Everything® Pregnancy Nutrition Book
Everything® Pregnancy Organizer, $15.00
Everything® Toddler Book
Everything® Tween Book
Everything® Twins, Triplets, and More Book

All Everything® books are priced at $12.95 or $14.95, unless otherwise stated. Prices subject to change without notice.

## PETS

Everything® Cat Book
Everything® Dachshund Book
Everything® Dog Book
Everything® Dog Health Book
Everything® Dog Training and Tricks Book
Everything® German Shepherd Book
Everything® Golden Retriever Book
Everything® Horse Book
Everything® Horseback Riding Book
Everything® Labrador Retriever Book
Everything® Poodle Book
Everything® Pug Book
Everything® Puppy Book
Everything® Rottweiler Book
Everything® Small Dogs Book
Everything® Tropical Fish Book
Everything® Yorkshire Terrier Book

## REFERENCE

Everything® Car Care Book
Everything® Classical Mythology Book
Everything® Computer Book
Everything® Divorce Book
Everything® Einstein Book
Everything® Etiquette Book, 2nd Ed.
Everything® Inventions and Patents Book
Everything® Mafia Book
Everything® Philosophy Book
Everything® Psychology Book
Everything® Shakespeare Book

## RELIGION

Everything® Angels Book
Everything® Bible Book
Everything® Buddhism Book
Everything® Catholicism Book
Everything® Christianity Book
Everything® Jewish History & Heritage Book
Everything® Judaism Book
Everything® Koran Book
Everything® Prayer Book
Everything® Saints Book

Everything® Torah Book
Everything® Understanding Islam Book
Everything® World's Religions Book
Everything® Zen Book

## SCHOOL & CAREERS

Everything® Alternative Careers Book
Everything® College Survival Book, 2nd Ed.
Everything® Cover Letter Book, 2nd Ed.
Everything® Get-a-Job Book
Everything® Guide to Starting and Running
    a Restaurant
Everything® Job Interview Book
Everything® New Teacher Book
Everything® Online Job Search Book
Everything® Paying for College Book
Everything® Practice Interview Book
Everything® Resume Book, 2nd Ed.
Everything® Study Book

## SELF-HELP

Everything® Dating Book, 2nd Ed.
Everything® Great Sex Book
Everything® Kama Sutra Book
Everything® Self-Esteem Book

## SPORTS & FITNESS

Everything® Fishing Book
Everything® Golf Instruction Book
Everything® Pilates Book
Everything® Running Book
Everything® Total Fitness Book
Everything® Weight Training Book
Everything® Yoga Book

## TRAVEL

Everything® Family Guide to Hawaii
Everything® Family Guide to Las Vegas,
    2nd Ed.
Everything® Family Guide to New York City,
    2nd Ed.
Everything® Family Guide to RV Travel &
    Campgrounds

Everything® Family Guide to the Walt Disney
    World Resort®, Universal Studios®,
    and Greater Orlando, 4th Ed.
Everything® Family Guide to Cruise Vacations
Everything® Family Guide to the Caribbean
Everything® Family Guide to Washington
    D.C., 2nd Ed.
Everything® Guide to New England
Everything® Travel Guide to the Disneyland
    Resort®, California Adventure®,
    Universal Studios®, and the
    Anaheim Area

## WEDDINGS

Everything® Bachelorette Party Book, $9.95
Everything® Bridesmaid Book, $9.95
Everything® Elopement Book, $9.95
Everything® Father of the Bride Book, $9.95
Everything® Groom Book, $9.95
Everything® Mother of the Bride Book, $9.95
Everything® Outdoor Wedding Book
Everything® Wedding Book, 3rd Ed.
Everything® Wedding Checklist, $9.95
Everything® Wedding Etiquette Book, $9.95
Everything® Wedding Organizer, $15.00
Everything® Wedding Shower Book, $9.95
Everything® Wedding Vows Book, $9.95
Everything® Weddings on a Budget Book,
    $9.95

## WRITING

Everything® Creative Writing Book
Everything® Get Published Book
Everything® Grammar and Style Book
Everything® Guide to Writing a Book Proposal
Everything® Guide to Writing a Novel
Everything® Guide to Writing Children's Books
Everything® Guide to Writing Research Papers
Everything® Screenwriting Book
Everything® Writing Poetry Book
Everything® Writing Well Book

Available wherever books are sold!
To order, call 800-258-0929, or visit us at *www.everything.com*
Everything® and everything.com® are registered trademarks of F+W Publications, Inc.